Learn and Play Out

D1423576

Do your children know how to grow potatoes, where to see a dragonfly or how to fire a rocket?

Are you one of the 82% of teachers who thinks their school isn't making as much use of their grounds as they should?

Do you know how to make the most of your outdoor teaching and learning spaces?

Learn and Play Out is an inspirational, accessible and pragmatic set of resources for making changes to primary school playgrounds in order to provide high-quality learning and play experiences. Drawing on Learning through Landscapes' experience in working with thousands of primary schools, it provides practical support to improve the use, design and management of your outdoor area.

More schools are seeing the benefits of their pupils spending longer periods of their school day outside, with research showing that this improves attainment, behaviour, motivation and self-esteem. For many schools however, the environment of their grounds does not meet the needs of their pupils. This toolkit helps them assess what they already have, work through what their needs are and inspires them to take the next steps forward to make physical and practical improvements to their grounds.

Featuring **a CD-ROM with a comprehensive and fully adaptable audit tool, plus activities and case study resources to support your work**, the handy toolkit provides:

- an overview of what your school grounds can do for you
- a step-by-step process to work through
- advice on how to involve the whole school community in planning changes
- guidance on managing your school grounds project
- practical activity ideas to involve children and adults.

This illustrated resource, which contains **over 140 full-colour photos**, will make it as easy as possible for teachers, parents and school governors to plan and manage a playground improvement project, involving children at the core of the work and linking the process and improved school grounds to curriculum learning objectives.

Learning through Landscapes (LTL) is the UK's national school grounds charity. LTL works with schools and Early Years settings, helping them to maximise the potential of their outdoor spaces for learning, play and wellbeing.

Learn and Play Out

How to develop your primary school's outside space

Learning through Landscapes

Routledge
Taylor & Francis Group

LONDON AND NEW YORK

First published 2014
by Routledge
2 Park Square, Milton Park, Abingdon, Oxon OX14 4RN

Simultaneously published in the USA and Canada
by Routledge
711 Third Avenue, New York, NY 10017

Routledge is an imprint of the Taylor & Francis Group, an informa business

© 2014 Learning through Landscapes

British Library Cataloguing in Publication Data
A catalogue record for this book is available from the British Library

Library of Congress Cataloging-in-Publication Data
Learn and play out: how to develop your primary school's outside space
learning through landscapes.
pages cm
1. Playgrounds. 2. School grounds.
LB3251.L43 2013
371.6'1–dc23
2012051116

ISBN: 978–0–415–65636–8 (pbk)

Typeset in Bembo
by Keystroke, Station Road, Codsall, Wolverhampton

Printed and bound in India by Replika Press Pvt. Ltd.

Contents

Preface   *vi*

Acknowledgements   *viii*

Introduction   *1*

Part 1: First steps   3

Part 2: The process of change   15

Part 3: Heading towards your vision   39

Part 4: Resources   77

Bibliography   *135*

Preface

The idea that outdoor learning and play can tackle many of the problems associated with the state of modern childhood is gaining support in the UK and elsewhere. Research around the world is shedding light not only on the importance to children of the natural world, regular activity and experiential learning and play, but also the role school grounds can have in addressing these issues.

- Less than 10% of children today play in natural spaces compared with 40% of adults when they were young (Natural England 2009) as woodlands, countryside and parks have become out of bounds to a generation of 'cotton-wool kids'. School grounds, however, can offer pupils contact with nature every day.
- 'Over half of the UK population could be obese by 2050' (Short Science Reviews 2007). In a survey of schools (Learning through Landscapes 2003) 85% of those that had improved their grounds reported increased active play and games. At the same time, 73% of schools reported that behaviour had improved, 64% claimed reduced bullying and 84% observed improved social interaction. Friendships made in the playground last for life and the social skills required throughout life are often forged in the school grounds. Creating places where positive relationships are built is vital.
- In a survey of schools (Learning through Landscapes 2003), 88% of those that had improved their grounds said it resulted in more creative learning and environmental awareness.

Despite all the evidence, however, 'Eight in ten teachers believe that their school is failing to make the most of their outside space for children' (Ipsos MORI 2008).

We want to ensure that every child benefits from outdoor learning and play as an integral part of their education. Over the past 22 years, we have worked with thousands of schools to help them rethink the design and use of their outside spaces. And now *Learn and Play Out* is enabling us to share our expertise and examples from our unrivalled experience even more widely. This resource will make it as easy as possible for teachers, parents and school governors to plan and manage a school grounds improvement project, involving children at the core of the work and linking the process and the improved school grounds to curriculum learning objectives and high-quality play experiences.

Learning through Landscapes

Learning through Landscapes is the UK charity dedicated to enhancing outdoor learning and play for children. Our vision is that every child benefits from stimulating outdoor learning and play in their education. We aim to enable children to connect with nature, be more active, be more engaged with their learning, develop their social skills and have fun!

We do this through three avenues:

- advocating the benefits of outdoor learning and play at school and preschool
- inspiring and enabling the design and development of outdoor environments to support children's development
- inspiring and enabling teachers and Early Years practitioners to develop the confidence, ideas and skills they need to make better use of outdoor spaces.

We are the leading UK charity specialising in outdoor learning and play in education. Our unrivalled knowledge and expertise is based on more than 20 years' experience of practical action and research. To find out more visit www.ltl.org.uk.

Acknowledgements

Learning through Landscapes would like to thank the following for helping to bring *Learn and Play Out* to life:

- Mary Jackson, writer, for sharing her extensive expertise, knowledge and experience in developing school grounds and ensuring this toolkit is comprehensive, realistic and inspirational.
- Tracey Godridge, writer and editor, for planning the toolkit, editing content and ensuring it is accessible and inspirational.
- All Learning through Landscapes staff for sharing their knowledge, experience, ideas and contacts.
- The pupils, staff and parents of the schools whose inspirational work and commitment to high-quality outdoor play have provided us with many of the ideas and activities featured here.

Introduction

This toolkit is about making physical change to your grounds in order to provide high-quality learning and play experiences for your pupils.

While a recent survey (Ipsos MORI 2010) showed that 97% of teachers believe that schools need to use their outside spaces effectively to enhance their pupils' development, a previous survey (Ipsos MORI 2008) showed that 82% do not agree that their own school is making as much use as it can of this valuable resource. There is clearly a gap between what teachers believe schools should be doing and what they are doing.

This toolkit is designed to help you think about and plan physical changes to your school grounds while making sure they will be right for *your* school, so that *your* pupils will be able to access better learning and play.

Your school is unique – you have a unique setting, unique pupils and unique teachers. There is, therefore, no one simple answer to how school grounds should be developed. What might be right for one school may not work in another. There are, however, some key principles that will help every school make the most of their grounds. Learning through Landscapes has been working with schools for over 22 years, and we have seen what works, and what doesn't. Key to success is taking an approach that is:

- **holistic.** Consider the whole site, all aspects of its use, and the wide range of needs of your school community and in particular your pupils. You may only be focusing on one aspect or area of your school grounds development but you will need to know how this fits into your wider plans to ensure success.
- **participative.** The wider and deeper your engagement from start to finish the more likely you are to come up with solutions that work for your school, the better the buy-in will be across the school community and the more likely it is that the changes will be fully used and cared for.
- **sustainable.** While this includes considering the materials and plants you use in making changes and how you manage the site, it is also important that changes are written into school policies and practices so that the project continues to benefit the school even when those involved in making the changes have moved on.

How to use this toolkit

This toolkit and the accompanying CD-ROM has everything you need to help ensure you make the most of your grounds by:

- helping you and your school agree on what you want to achieve from your grounds developments and why
- ensuring that you are able to engage your pupils and wider community throughout the process of developing your grounds
- expanding your vision so that your school grounds developments are innovative and creative.

The CD-ROM contains all the material that you will find in *Part 4: Resources* (see below) including an audit tool, cases studies and a range of activities. By having these materials in hard copy and on the CD-ROM you will be able to repeat the audit over the year and print and share all the activity ideas, case studies and images as you need them.

Here is a summary of each section:

Part 1: First steps. This explains more about why school grounds matter, how to overcome some of the common issues and barriers that arise, and how to get started.

Part 2: The process of change. This takes you through the process of change – a simple four-part structure that will help you plan and deliver your project. At all stages it is important that you look at the **use, design** and **management** of your grounds. In this way, you may discover that changes to how you use and manage your grounds may be as important as making physical changes. The likelihood is that you will make changes to all three aspects so you will need to think about how these interact to get the best possible solutions for your school. Here you will also find links to resources in *Part 4* that will help you through the process.

Part 3: Heading towards your vision. This looks at 11 key themes, with inspirational images, that you may wish to focus on when developing your grounds. This section is to be used when you have decided which themes you want to develop in your grounds. You may have a clear idea of this before you start the project but by completing the audit you will find out in more detail where you truly excel and where you need to improve. The themes featured are common to many school grounds projects. Most schools will find that they want to address more than one of these in the long term, but may wish to start with one. For each theme there is information about why this aspect of school grounds is important, how you can make it work in your own grounds, top tips, links to further information and support and images to inspire.

Part 4: Resources. This offers a range of resources to help your project. As explained above, all the resources that are in the book are also available on the accompanying CD-ROM for you to download and use as many times as you wish, including:

- an **audit tool** designed to help you find out what you are doing well in your school grounds and what you could focus on next
- **11 inspirational case studies with images** from schools that have focused particularly on one of the key themes identified in *Part 3: Heading towards your vision*
- **24 activity sheets** providing you with a range of ways to gather information and implement your plans at each stage of the process.

Part 1: First steps

There are many important reasons for starting a school grounds project – and understanding the benefits that can be brought to your pupils, your staff and your community will provide you with the motivation to get started, and keep going.

Why develop your school grounds?

Two-thirds of the school estate is outside space but it is often a wasted resource. Used to their fullest advantage, the benefits of these precious spaces extend beyond play. Well-designed outside spaces provide a stimulating educational resource that can bring teaching – in its widest sense – alive, which in turn brings benefits to children, teachers and the wider community.

The benefits for children

Many people intrinsically understand the importance of the outdoors for children – they know that children need to get outside for their physical and mental health and general wellbeing. However, in many schools the way the grounds are designed and managed does not reflect this. While the inside of the building displays pupils' work and items created by the pupils, often the same cannot be said of the outside. This sends messages to the pupils about the relative importance of the two spaces, especially as a place for real learning.

School grounds provide pupils with spaces to learn, to play, to socialise and be active. They are the place where friendships are secured but also where bullying can take place. They also provide great opportunities for pupils to contribute to the school community – through the process of developing and managing spaces and features within them. Schools where pupils have engaged with this process report improved behaviour, raised self-esteem, better social interaction, reduced incidents of bullying and improved academic achievement (Learning through Landscapes in London 2003).

Recent research from around the globe has shown the importance of teaching outside in general and in the school grounds specifically and just a small selection of that research is given on the following pages. More specific information related to key themes can be found in *Part 3: Heading towards your vision* and on the research pages of the Learning through Landscapes (LTL) website at www.ltl.org.uk.

Did you know...

When learning in the natural environment students:

- perform better in reading, mathematics, science and social studies
- show greater motivation for studying science.

King's College London (2011)

A school's grounds is the one common outside place the vast majority of children have access to and which they can spend as much as, and in many cases more than, 25% of their time in during the week. And it is often one place they feel safe. It is therefore vital that these spaces become places that are suitable for children to spend time in, that they stimulate their curiosity and enthusiasm for learning and that they enable our children to live active and healthy lives.

Research shows that when developing their grounds:

- 65% schools reported an improved attitude to learning
- 73% said behaviour had improved
- 64% reported reduced bullying
- 84% reported improved social interaction
- 85% said that healthy active play had increased.

Learning through Landscapes (2003)

The benefits for teachers

Developing outside spaces can provide teachers with a wide range of resources and environments for teaching in creative ways. This can complement and help build on work inside and provide a different dimension for lesson activities, helping to engage and stretch their pupils. Staff develop different relationships with pupils outside and they are able to observe pupils in a space away from the classroom.

Did you know...

- Teachers benefit from Learning in Natural Environments (LINE).
- They become more enthusiastic about teaching and bringing innovative teaching strategies to the classroom.

Natural England (2012)

Enhancing play spaces outside has also been shown to have a direct link to positive pupil behaviour with pupils settling down in lessons better after a positive playtime, making teaching more productive and enjoyable.

The school grounds also link in with a range of existing initiatives that the school might be involved in, e.g. Eco Schools, Health Promoting Schools and Healthy Schools,

Rights Respecting Schools, Active Learning, Education for Sustainable Development, Learning outside the Classroom and the Creative Curriculum.

The benefits for the wider community

School grounds projects can help develop school–home links as children, parents and even grandparents get involved in the process. There is also potential for generating business for local companies and individuals. Projects can bring positive publicity to the school and the development and use of the grounds can become a positive feature of HMIE or Ofsted reports, both of which can also encourage parents to look positively at the school.

The community can use the grounds for a range of activities and events such as camping, festivals, sport, car boot sales and farmers markets, learning new skills and outdoor performances.

Parents see that school grounds are important, as the research findings in the *Did you know . . .* box show, and this should be considered if looking at creating a school on a site that does not have good outdoor facilities.

> ## Did you know...
>
> - 98% of parents think that outside play is essential or desirable to school life.
> - 94% stated that sports fields were essential or desirable in school life.
>
> YouGov (2010)

Think positive – overcoming hurdles!

If the prospect of developing your school grounds sounds daunting, remember that even the smallest step – from putting up a bird box to growing potatoes in a planter – can make a difference and inspire everyone towards further changes. And while their will be hurdles along the way, none of them are insurmountable. Here is a look at some key challenges – and how to deal with them.

Funding

Lack of funding is one of the most common barriers cited to making changes to the school grounds. First, it is important to bear in mind many changes can be made for a low cost – and some may be completely free. Second, often skills and time are equally if not more important than cash.

Think about what is needed for the project to be successful. Can you ask, for example, members of your school community (teachers, parents, governors etc.) to donate something – from a packet of seeds or an old pair of wellies to expert advice on planning permission? Look too at local businesses, and even those businesses parents work for and those that supply your school in some way. Many have a 'Corporate Social Responsibility' (CSR) policy and may be able to offer materials, money or people to help you with your project. Others may have end-of-line or end-of-season products they are happy to donate. Your local Business Education Partnership or Scottish Business in the Community organisation may be able to make a match between your needs and what local companies can offer.

Contrary to popular belief, there is a host of funding available for schools to access. From a modest seating area to a major landscaping project, developing a short funding plan will help you identify where the funding is available from and how you can access it. The basic information your plan should include is:

- What funding is needed – what types of activities, how much and when?
- Where will funds come from?
- What activities need to happen to raise funds, when do they need to happen and who will do them?

The world of fundraising changes frequently as trends in funding priorities shift and funders objectives move. For up-to-date information about where to access funding sign up to LTL's FREE subscription service for monthly fundraising recommendations and advice (www.ltl.org.uk).

Here are a few top tips to inspire you:

- Always identify your project outcomes first. This will help you shape your funding application. The Big Lottery Fund has some great advice about outcomes and measuring impact (www.biglotteryfund.org.uk).
- Consider allowing some community access, for example, a parents meeting space, a venue for community days or a community growing space will attract a different type of funder.
- Most large companies will have programmes to support their local community. Put a call out to parents – do they work for an employer who can contribute? Or are they the boss?
- As with the design, think about fundraising in sections. Some funders cap the total project size that they are willing to support (even if they are only funding part of it).
- It doesn't have to be money – can the local DIY store donate some equipment, can parents and pupils help with making the changes, have you checked out your local recycling centre? Where funders ask you to demonstrate match funding this 'in-kind' support can be included.
- Wherever you get funding or resources from, don't forget to thank your funders. Invite them to see what you are doing and keep them up to date with what is going on. It is generally easier to keep a funder than get a new one, so showing them that you are making the most of their money will help you with any further plans.

Money makers

Fundraising activities can be fun, and linking them to your specific project can engage even more people in its success. Holding a gardeners' question time at school or running a session on growing seedlings to sell to parents are just two ways of raising funds. Go with your strengths as a school and get everyone on board to make the most of your fundraising activities.

Vandalism

Considering potential vandalism is important. Only you will know what your area is like and whether you are likely to have unwanted visitors on your site who may do damage. However, many schools find they overestimate the damage that will take place if they create something new in their grounds and the experience of schools across the country is that making improvements to their grounds can often help reduce the problem rather than increase it. The more somewhere looks cared for the more likely people are to look after it. When a space looks rundown then vandalism is more likely to occur. So make sure that any vandalism that does take place is cleared up and repaired as quickly as possible. If you can identify people who can be called on quickly to help in different situations, then this makes this process even quicker.

In addition, involving pupils in the whole development process will also help create a sense of ownership and an understanding of what it takes to make positive spaces. This can also encourage siblings to take more care of the grounds, some of whom might be the unplanned visitors to the site. Involving students from the local secondary school or college, youth clubs and also local youth services may mean that these young people also understand and respect what has been happening.

If there is a problem in your grounds your pupils could write to the press to highlight the issue and drum up local support. Make friends with your neighbours too. Many schools are surrounded by housing so do ask local residents to keep a look out and report any problems they see.

Money makers

Think about the materials you use in your grounds. Don't just go for the cheapest version of something. Consider using materials that are hard-wearing and difficult to destroy. This is particularly important when you are looking at storage.

The first instinct of many schools concerned about vandalism is to erect high fencing around their site, install security cameras and not allow any informal use out of school hours. There can be good reasons for incorporating these elements into the way you manage the site but schools have often found that a more open approach can be just as effective. For example, if you invite local people to use the site in the evening then you are likely to put off unwanted visitors who might do damage. And while it is essential for the school to consider the safeguarding of its pupils they need to feel safe without feeling 'fenced in'. Having good visibility across the site is one way to help that happen.

Getting the balance between security and making a welcoming space is important, and for each school the solution will be different. Below are some things to consider when making your decisions:

- How effective is your existing system?
- Are there places within the grounds where there are particular issues?
- Is there good visibility across the site? Or are there particular places where this is a problem? (this is different from creating hiding spaces and dens which you may wish to encourage).
- Do you need high fencing all around the site or are there alternatives?

- Would planting be an effective security measure instead of permanent fencing along any stretches of your site? Thorny hedging can be even more difficult to get through than a fence.
- Consider your entrances and exits – who uses these, who could use these, are they open or secure and if the latter are there specific times when this is the case?
- Consider the materials and design of features in your grounds to ensure they are more vandal-proof.
- Be ready to repair and make changes to reduce problems in the future.

Staff resistance

It is not always possible to get every member of staff to be as enthusiastic about your school grounds project as you are but there are things you can do to ensure that they are on-board at least in principle, and hopefully in practice.

First, there may be good reason why staff are not enthusiastic and it is worth acknowledging this. It might be that a project has been tried before and not been a success, e.g. a pond put in a far corner then not looked after so it doesn't get used, or a project was started but money was not forthcoming and plans had to be reduced or cancelled. There could also be personal reasons for lack of enthusiasm; not everyone likes to be outside while others may be uncertain about taking classes outside – whether through concerns about control or a worry about lack of knowledge.

Staff supervising playtimes might be concerned about using different approaches to play, while whoever manages the site might be worried that about adding to their workload.

Some ways to get staff involved can include:

- sharing examples of other schools – see the case studies and images in *Part 4: Resources* and watch videos from the LTL YouTube channel
- visiting other schools that have undertaken similar projects
- providing appropriate training – CPD to support teachers working outdoors is available from Learning through Landscapes as well as other outdoor education providers
- team teaching or shadowing colleagues teaching outside
- making sure they are consulted about how they may need to manage any changes once they have occurred.

Safety and risk

Safety is obviously a very important consideration for schools – both in the creation of new outdoor features and also in their use – so it is important that the grounds are considered within the schools health and safety policy and that good records are kept of any risk assessments or risk-benefit analysis you complete.

The good news is that the vast majority of activities undertaken in school grounds, and the equipment used to enable them, are very safe. Even elements that give the impression of being dangerous can be safely incorporated into school grounds if planned well.

When creating new features consider current safety standards. Any supplier of new equipment will have knowledge of these and are likely to design their equipment to comply with them. In addition RoSPA (www.rospa.com) and the Health and Safety Executive (www.hse.gov.uk) provide guidance that will help you make decisions for your site. The positioning of features is also important – so that they can be safely used without interference from or to others.

When a new feature is to be added to the site you will need to think about who is to undertake the work and when the work is to be done. Some jobs will need experts to undertake them whilst others could be carried out by unskilled labour, but both will need to be looked at in terms of hazards and risks. Some schools will want their pupils to observe the changes made by others; others will feel that they need to undertake major works during the holidays. Some work may be undertaken with a specialist working with pupils and this too should be risk assessed. Consider the pros and cons of each approach before deciding which route to go down.

While safety is important it is also vital that children experience risk and challenge – so that they come to understand where their limits lie and where they have to be more careful. They will naturally undertake their own risk assessment as they view a feature and the more obvious the risk – e.g. something high, something challenging to climb across – the more likely they are to assess the risks correctly. This skill they will take beyond the school gates as they develop self-confidence and courage to try something new. If children are overly protected they do not learn these skills and could potentially put themselves in more dangerous situations. School grounds, where children feel safe and hazards are managed, are therefore a great place for children to learn about risk.

While schools will be familiar with the risk assessment process they may not be so familiar with the ideas of risk-benefit analysis and dynamic risk assessment. The latter is all about reassessing the risk within an activity as it progresses. Staff have to make decisions about their pupils as they undertake different activities and these decisions change as they come across something new. This can be particularly true during unstructured play where materials and equipment may be used in creative ways by pupils, ways that adults might not have thought about before. If a member of staff is aware that these changes might take place they can be ready to react in an appropriate way.

A risk-benefit analysis is a positive way of considering an activity and, as the name suggests, it helps you think about balancing its benefits to its risks. The greater the benefit of an activity the higher the risks you might be willing to take. Play England (www.playengland.org.uk) in *Managing Risk in Play Provision; Implementation Guide* and PLAYLINK (www.playlink.org) both provide information and examples about undertaking a risk-benefit analysis of play and these can be readily applied to the range of activities that might take place within the school grounds.

Weather

Britain is famed for its obsession with the weather – and it does make a difference to how often you might go outside. However, there are some schools that manage to defy the odds and regularly take outdoor lessons throughout the year. So how do they do it?

There is a saying that there is no such thing as bad weather, just inappropriate clothing – so some schools make sure that there is a store of wet-weather gear that can be lent out when needed. Other schools encourage pupils to bring in their own wellington boots etc. and have wellie-racks to store them on during the day as well as areas assigned for drying clothes.

When given a choice, pupils will regularly choose to go outside when it is wet. If they are kept inside at break- and lunchtimes there is often an impact on their behaviour in lessons that follow. Therefore make sure staff also have appropriate clothing to go outside in all weathers so that pupils can have the option to be outside. Collect resources that can be used in the rain – creating a resources box that can be developed over time. Let parents know that there is a policy in your school to go outside when it is wet so they, or the school, can make sure the pupils have the appropriate clothing.

Having some covered space outside means that classes can gather outdoors, or have more play and lessons in the fresh air even when it is raining. This might be an awning or pergola directly outside classrooms or meeting spaces further into the school grounds. This type of feature also provides shaded and sheltered spaces for use on sunny or windy days.

Make the most of the weather when you can. The beauty of using the school grounds is that they are always accessible. This means that when there is a break in the weather you can nip outside for a few minutes. This does require teachers to be flexible in the way they work, but can lead to some creative and stimulating teaching.

The sun can be just as much of a problem as rain. Many school grounds have very little shade so being outside for extended periods of time can be an issue. Shade can be created in many ways; trees are an excellent long-term addition as they provide the shade in the summer months when it is most needed. Permanent structures can make a huge difference but can be costly. Using sheets, tarpaulins, teepees, dens, etc. can be a good temporary alternative for creating shade for play and learning, with more permanent features added as money allows.

Some sites can be very windy and it is worth undertaking a survey of your site to find out where the windy and sheltered spots are. Planting can help mitigate against wind but needs to be undertaken with care as it is possible to create more problems if put in the wrong place. The location of buildings can also impact on air movement around the site, so if you are having new building work, make sure this element is discussed with the designer.

In the winter make the most of frost, snow and ice. Whilst more care needs to be taken in these conditions they provide exciting potential for learning and play. This is where using a risk-benefit approach will help you decide how to deal with difficult conditions and where creative teaching staff will help your pupils experience the outdoors in innovative ways.

Parental concerns

If you are changing your school grounds or the way they are used you may find that some parents are concerned. They may be worried, for example, that being outside their children will get muddy or that having lessons outside isn't 'real' learning.

During a grounds development project make sure you keep parents well informed about what is happening, that they are represented on the management team and have opportunities to contribute to the changes being made. At the start of the project share the concept with parents – maybe as part of a PTA meeting. Use relevant video clips from our YouTube channel (www.youtube.com/schoolgroundsuk) or create posters using the images and case studies in *Part 4: Resources* toolkit or from the internet.

Introducing new forms of play may worry parents. They may see elements that their children could fall off, loose equipment they might hurt each other with or ways their clothes might get damaged. A good way to address these issues is to invite them in to the school to watch their children play, or even play with them. This is the best kind of risk-benefit analysis, where it is clear that the benefits outweigh the risks just from watching play happen. If you want to show them these benefits before you have made changes then you can take them to see similar resources elsewhere or ask them to think about what they enjoyed about play when they were children. You can also bring in loose equipment, such as sticks, stones, sheets and ropes for the children to play with or for parents to try out before you make physical changes to your site to give them a feel of what is to come.

Different changes will elicit different issues from parents and each needs to be responded to accordingly. However, some general principles can be applied – keep parents informed, invite them in to see what is happening and get them involved and experiencing the new approach themselves.

Finding help

The good news is that there is lots of help out there! Some of it comes for free while other help will require some investment, which may well be worth making to ensure that you get the best possible grounds for your school and that those grounds get used to their full potential.

You will find a list of useful national organisations in *Part 4: Resources – More useful organisations*. Some ideas of the types of people who might be able to help are listed below:

- Members of your school community who may include gardeners, artists, designers, builders, accountants, fundraisers. See *Part 4: Resources – Activity 19: Skills audit template*.
- Local companies – good to approach for funding, for resources and for volunteer help.
- the voluntary sector – some of these organisations may have initiatives you can be involved with that are fully funded while you may need to pay for other services. The type of help you can get could include information, guidance and support on wildlife and biodiversity, sustainability, play, gardening and the arts. You may also get support from local organisations such as Rotary, Scouts and Guides, or an allotment society.
- Your local authority may be able to provide you with support. Both educational and environmental departments of local authorities will have staff who work in school grounds. They might provide help with legal guidance, specific areas of need such as arboriculture or providing training for staff in how to use the grounds for teaching and learning or for play and recreation.
- If you are undertaking a large-scale project you may wish to employ a landscape architect. The Landscape Institute (*see Part 4: Resources – More useful organisations*) has a list of registered practices and you can search their list online for a practice in your local area that has experience of working with schools. There are several practices that also have long links with Learning through Landscapes, and some designers who have received Learning through Landscapes training.
- Learning through Landscapes has accredited a number of school grounds professionals throughout the UK, some working on their own or in small companies, others working for NGOs, some based in local authorities and some in design practices. Choosing someone who is LTL accredited means you know that person understands the process outlined in this toolkit and has been assessed by LTL in this approach.

Getting your project started

Sharing the concept

It is important that you let everyone know that you are wanting to make changes in your grounds. Consider who needs to know and the different methods you can use to do this.

- **Pupils** could be informed through an assembly, through the school council, through lessons and noticeboards.
- **Staff** (teaching and non-teaching) can be informed through staff meetings and governors through governor meetings.
- **Parents** might be informed through PTA meetings, newsletters or noticeboards at the entrance to the school, or via their children.

You can use resources such as the case studies and images in *Part 4: Resources*, from the LTL website (www.ltl.org.uk), videos from our YouTube channel (www.youtube.com/schoolgroundsuk) or visit other schools that have undertaken similar work.

Use your own school website, newsletter and noticeboards to let everyone know that something is about to get going and make sure you continue to keep everyone informed as the project progresses.

Setting up a management team

We suggest you set up a management team to run your project. There are a number of good reasons for this:

- the more ideas contributed to the project the better
- having a range of users involved will help you see issues from different perspectives
- different people will bring different skills – someone may be good at writing application forms whilst another is good at coming up with ideas
- if the main lead person leaves, there is a better chance that the project will continue.

Make sure your management team has a good representation of people within it – if you can run it at a time that pupils can attend even better. However, if you have to have separate meetings for adults and children do make sure they can feed into each other's groups so that everyone's voices are heard. There will certainly be some things the pupils will know more about that the adults.

Maintaining momentum

Your school grounds project will go through times when lots is happening and other times when you will feel like you have got stuck! So how do you ensure that you get through the slow phases without losing everyone's support and enthusiasm?

- Try to balance out the long-term project with small, quicker changes that can be made on the way. Have an action plan that outlines when things are going to take place – this will also help you see when quiet times are likely to occur. You cannot always move at the same rate, some changes will need time to plan, fund and implement so having some low-cost, simple changes up your sleeve can ensure everyone continues to see things changing. Set aside a small budget to enable these items to continue when you have pauses in your main project changes.

- Try to make changes that are visible beyond the school community so that everyone knows you are serious about your project and make sure you don't make changes that restrict what you can do in the future.
- Keep everyone up to date with what is going on – through newsletters, the internet, noticeboards and meetings. Have regular updates in assembly and make the grounds a regular agenda item on staff, school council and governor meetings.
- Set dates for your school grounds management team well ahead of time so that you always have a good turnout and make sure you have a comprehensive agenda for the meetings as well as a chairperson. Minutes should be communicated back to all concerned.
- Celebrate the changes you make and organise events in the grounds so that they get used as soon as possible and so that the changes are valued.

Measuring success

There are a range of tools in the resources section to help you measure the success of your project. There are three aspects of measuring success:

- **Monitoring** – collecting and recording and observing development on a systematic basis over time.
- **Evaluation** – investigating and reflecting on the nature, quality, impact and effectiveness of developments.
- **Review** – studying the developments and outcomes observed in order to make decisions regarding future strategies and actions.

Together these can help you:

- know what is/is not being achieved
- identify areas for future improvement
- demonstrate your achievements to funders
- publicise your achievements internally or externally.

You will see that the process of change this toolkit takes you through has four stages – at each step you should incorporate evaluation activities and not just leave this until the end of your project.

Stage 1: Where are we now? This is the stage where you will you will get your baseline data. This should include 'before' images so that you can demonstrate what you have done when you have made changes. You should also have collected a lot of information about how the grounds are used before the changes as well as how people felt about them at the start of your project.

Stage 2: Where do we want to be? This stage of the project focuses on your aims – what do you want to achieve so at the end of your project you are able to compare to your original aims.

Stages 3 and 4: How can we get there? and Making the changes. During these stages monitoring takes priority over evaluation – so make sure you keep good records of what you are planning to do.

Once you have completed these four stages, look again at Stage 1: Where are we now? This is the time to repeat the information gathering you did at the start of the process so that you can see what you have achieved. Also, refer to your aims to make sure you are heading in the right direction.

Part 2: The process of change

A structured approach to planning changes to your grounds will help you use resources – money and time – effectively, and ensure the changes meet the needs of your school now and in the future.

The 'process of change' recommended by Learning through Landscapes is based on an approach used by architects, landscape designers and engineers: survey it, analyse it, design it and manage it. Over 22 years' experience working with schools has enabled Learning through Landscapes to adapt this method to suit the specific circumstances of schools.

Whether you are starting a school grounds project from scratch, have made a few changes or transformed parts of your grounds already, this 'process of change' will help you take the next steps. It provides a simple structure to help you think through all the different elements you need to consider – whatever stage you are at – by helping you ask vital questions and ensuring you don't jump in too quickly with solutions that might not be best in the long term.

Your project may be a major programme or a series of smaller, incremental changes, but whatever your strategy you should take a whole-site approach – thinking about how all the different areas and aspects of your grounds and school community work together, and how any changes will fit into your overall plans for development in the years to come, even if you ultimately make changes to those ideas along the way.

The process has four stages, and forms a full circle, so when you have completed Stage 4, you return to Stage 1. It is designed this way for two reasons – first, to see if you have achieved what you set out to do, and second, to help you set off on the next stage of your project. Most schools with wonderful outdoor spaces started with small steps and developed their grounds over several years. For this reason, a school grounds project is often never completed, and this is a good thing – it means that every generation of children that passes through the school can make their own mark on the grounds, develop a sense of ownership of the site and leave something great for the following cohort of pupils.

As you work through the process, you will need to think about three aspects of your grounds: **use, design** and **management**.

- **Use – what should pupils be able to experience, learn and develop?** This involves deciding what kind of experiences you want pupils to have outside; how this links to your overall educational aims and objectives; any curriculum links and the use of materials or resources; the school's approach to teaching and learning outdoors; the role of adults.
- **Design – what will your outdoor area look and feel like? What features and resources will it contain?** This involves observing the shapes and sizes of the different physical spaces; identifying existing or potential uses; noting major features of the landscape, such as large areas of planting, main routes through and access points; establishing whether you'll need to use a professional designer.
- **Management – how will your aims, values and organisation support the development and use of the outdoor area?** This involves addressing any gaps in

existing policy and procedures; identifying areas for improvement, such as in-service training needs, risk assessments, budgetary reviews, improvements to documentation; examining priorities. These three aspects link up. For example, you may decide that you need child-friendly storage and this would support:

  o Improvements to the curriculum – the children have ready access to equipment for mathematical and numeracy development (use).

  o Improving the physical features and overall design of the site (design).

  o A change of policy and staff approach to enable children to access equipment independently (management).

● Or your plan may identify that a workshop on the use of outdoors is needed for staff and parents to:

  o Increase understanding of the importance of the use of outdoors to children's overall health, wellbeing and learning (use) which in turn will lead to . . .

  o . . . the creation of a new outdoor learning and play policy (management).

You will also find that many of the activities you undertake throughout the process of change will also help you deliver different aspects of the curriculum. This might be measuring your site for maths, writing questionnaires for English, undertaking survey work for science or geography, or maybe design and technology in creating new features.

Learning from others

Included in *Part 4: Resources* are ten case studies of how schools have tackled improvements to their grounds. Each school is unique and the case studies do not represent a comprehensive set of ideas, but offer tried and tested methods for the successful development of school grounds. Reading the case studies should help you start to plan how you could structure and manage your own project.

Stage 1: Where are we now?

This stage of the 'process of change' looks at what your grounds currently have to offer, including:

- **Use.** How are your grounds currently used for learning and play?
- **Design.** What is the existing layout and features of your grounds?
- **Management.** What current policies and practices do you have in place for your grounds?

Your first step is to complete the *Audit* in *Part 4: Resources* to help you evaluate your current practice and provision. There are a range of questions and a summary table to which you should add your findings.

You can collect the answers to these questions in a variety of ways. There are a range of tools to help listed in the *Tools to help* box below and included in *Part 4: Resources* which are designed to help you get answers. You do not have to use all these tools – feel free to select the ideas you feel are most useful to you. You also could use staff meetings or curriculum planning meetings to gather information, and you may have other methods that you know will work better in your school, or specific skills and techniques within your school for finding the answers to the same questions – so be creative and use your ideas too, or adapt the ideas we have given you to suit your school community.

At this stage, resist the urge to identify solutions – the time for solutions will come later, especially as you may find one solution meets several needs and this might be missed if you address issues separately.

Make sure you have a project folder to keep all the information you gather together so it is easy to access as you move through the process of change. Not only will the information you gather now help you head off in the right direction, it will also provide you with your baseline data that will help you establish the impact of your project.

Staff involvement and staff development are also key ingredients in making a success of the project. Make sure you look regularly at how your outdoor developments are going to reflect the values and aims of your school as a whole. Have you, for example, taken account of any action points from your most recent inspection report?

Tools to help

Audit	Using overlays
Observation	Using a plan with images
Creating a breaktime diary	Creating a model of your site
Tour of your grounds	What do *you* think?
Collecting baseline data	Let's talk

Use

The first section of the *Audit* in *Part 4: Resources* will help you get an overview of how you use your grounds. Furthermore, it will encourage you to look in detail at how you are *currently* using your grounds. What, for example, are your pupils currently able to learn and experience outdoors? The first step to improving experiences in your grounds is to take a good look at how they are currently used for learning, play and their wider development. This is important for a number of reasons. First, developing how you use what you already have may be more effective than making physical changes. There will always be an aspect of provision that can be developed straight away, and small improvements give everyone confidence and motivation to go further. Second, you may already be doing some things well in your school grounds – this might be teaching outside, community use, successful playtimes or encouraging wildlife to visit. Looking at what your grounds currently offer, and how they are currently used, will clarify how far you want to go (your vision).

One of the best ways for seeing how the grounds are used is simply by observation. You can observe the grounds at different times of day, focus on different areas, or watch individuals or small groups to see how they use the grounds over a given period of time. See *Part 4: Resources – Activity 1: Observation* for different ideas using observation on how to gather information about what is going on in your grounds. Get the pupils involved too – *Creating a breaktime diary* is a great activity to find out how children use the playgrounds. Walking around the site can also prompt people's thoughts, as can simple questionnaires and discussions. There are a number of ways you can organise these – see *Part 4: Resources – Activity 3: Tour of your grounds, Activity 4: What do you think?* and *Activity 5: Let's talk.*

As part of the *Audit* you will be looking at how much teaching you take outside and which subject areas are most often taken outdoors. From this you may decide to take a look at how to increase the level of teaching outside. Keeping a record of when and where you take lessons outside at this stage in the process will allow you to compare changes at the end.

During this process it is vital that you identify the views of your pupils and staff. Pupils are the experts on your site – they are outside using it every day and know, for example, where you would go to be out of the wind and which areas are used for different activities. They will also have quite strong views about what they like and don't like so it is important they have the opportunity to express their feelings as part of this project. Resources available in *Part 4* specifically designed to help you gather their perspectives include the activities: *Tour of your grounds, Let's talk, What do you think?* and *Collecting baseline data.*

Design

The second section of the *Audit* in *Part 4: Resources* will help you get an overview of how your grounds are currently designed as well as encouraging you to look at them in detail. The design of your grounds impacts on how they are used and how pupils feel about them – which in turn affects how they behave in them and look after them. Surveying and gathering good information on what your grounds look and feel like, and what resources and features they contain will reduce the risk of making inappropriate changes. A survey will also help everyone familiarise themselves with the space and start to develop a strong sense of ownership of future developments. For ideas on what you need to include see the *Information to collect for your design survey* box below.

Information to collect for your design survey

Base plan. There are several things in your grounds that cannot be changed, or are very unlikely to change. These are the features you need to add to your base plan if they are not on there already. This might include:

- buildings
- playgrounds and car parks
- footpaths
- mature, healthy trees
- boundaries – fences, hedges and walls
- gates
- entrances and exits to the site from outside and from the building
- underground services and overhead cables.

Overlays. There will also be features that you may decide to change in some way. These should be added to one of your overlays. You could have one overlay for things unlikely to change, and one for things you want to change. This might include:

- smaller or unhealthy trees and shrubs
- pitch, court and playground markings
- seating and meeting places
- wildlife areas or growing areas
- art works.

Record this information on a base plan of your site. You should be able to get one from your local authority – at least in electronic form. The Ordnance Survey (see *Part 4: Resources – More useful organisations*) also have a system allowing schools to access digital maps that you can annotate, draw on and print out. This is available to all primary schools for a reasonable fee. The larger the plan the easier it will be to work with – so, if possible, get one A2 size.

Once you have a base plan, you can start to record what is currently found on your site. Many surveying tasks can be undertaken by staff and children during their regular times outdoors. For more on how to set about surveying your site see *Part 4: Resources – Activity 6: Collecting baseline data*.

Mark on your base plan everything that is unlikely to change – buildings, hard standings, mature trees, entrances and exits to your site and building – and what condition they are in, since poorly maintained grounds can create health and safety hazards and prevent their use. You will also need to record features that are hidden from view, such as the underground services.

To keep your base plan clean so that you can use it to record different types and levels of information, use overlays (tracing paper or something you can see through and draw on laid over the top of your base plan) to mark your findings on. For more information on using overlays see *Part 4 Resources – Activity 7: Using overlays*.

A view from above

Giving pupils, staff and parents a chance to input is vital to making successful changes. One way to do this is to create an overview – either using a plan and/or a model – of your site.

- **Using a plan with images.** Creating a giant plan of your site is a great way for everyone to be able to add ideas and comments. Add images to help ensure everyone is clear on what they are looking at. As you go through the process of change you can change the images to match the stage you are at. This is a good way for everyone in the school to see how the project is progressing. For this stage in the process, 'Where are we now?', involve pupils by getting them to draw or photograph the different spaces and features; they can then annotate their images with an explanation as to whether that space or feature is important to them.
- **Creating a model of your site.** Using a physical model of your site will also allow the school community to comment and suggest changes. Lay the largest version you can of your base plan out in a space where it can be easily viewed. Pupils can then make copies or representations of existing features and locate them on the plan. As the plan progresses, these features can be changed and relocated.

Management

The third section of the *Audit* in *Part 4: Resources* will help you get an overview of how you manage your grounds, as well as encouraging you to look in detail at the policies and practices that inform the management of your school grounds. For example, how well do your aims, values and organisation support the development and use of the school grounds? Review how information about the value of outdoors is shared at present and where there are gaps in policies and procedures relating to outdoors. This will help you to make improvements to all your school's paperwork associated with outdoors. This development process may be a difficult journey that has to be approached sensitively to allow old habits and ways of working to be slowly reviewed, changed and improved.

As with every other aspect of your developments outdoors it will be important to consult widely about changes to documentation to ensure that it accurately reflects the philosophy of your school and all those involved in it, rather than being a 'rubber stamping' exercise that is unlikely to be fully implemented.

Management: Gathering your thoughts

The list below will help you gather your thoughts when working through the audit.

Policies. Do you have a policy about the use and management of your grounds? When was it adopted? Who was involved in the development of it? Does it need reviewing?

Risk assessment. Do you include school grounds in your risk assessments or risk-benefit analysis? When was the last outdoor risk assessment carried out? Have you addressed the issues it identified? Who has responsibility for carrying out risk assessments?

Finances. Are school grounds included in your annual budget? Do you have a budget for ongoing outdoor maintenance tasks? Do you set aside money for future developments as well as seasonal replenishments, such as seeds and sand? Do you set aside a budget for outdoor clothing for staff and children?

Site management and maintenance. Who undertakes all the different aspects of management and maintenance of the site? How successfully is this being completed? This will help you with the later stages of your project. If you have an external contractor responsible for grounds management tasks, have you reviewed the contract recently to ensure it is being adhered to?

Staff. Does anyone on the senior management team have a specific responsibility for outdoors? Do job descriptions include an expectation that staff will be outdoors? Do staff interviews include questions about the adult role outdoors? How do you ensure that staff are adequately protected from extreme weather conditions?

Parents. How do you share ongoing information about outdoors with parents? Do parents value your outdoor space and the opportunities it offers their children? Are parents involved in the care and development of your outdoor space?

Publicity. Is the value, use and management of outdoors stated clearly in your prospectus and newsletters? Do you display photographs of children using the outdoor space? Do you hold events outdoors?

Records. How do you include outdoors in your planning and assessment documentation? Do you observe and assess children's play and learning outdoors? Do you use your observations of children outdoors to inform your future planning? Do you include examples of learning outdoors in children's assessment records?

Continuous professional development and training. How often does outdoor learning feature in your staff meetings and training days? How often does it feature on individual staff members' performance reviews or personal training plans? Do staff get access to external conferences or training opportunities on outdoor learning?

Once you have completed the first three sections of the *Audit* to give yourself an overview of your grounds you will need to undertake the more focused sections. There are 11 of these sections, each looking at a theme that is common for schools to address in their school grounds projects. You may already have a good idea of what your strengths and weaknesses are but completing the *Audit* will help you focus in more closely and may highlight aspects that you had not considered previously.

By the end of this stage you will have:

- completed your school grounds audit
- gathered information on the way the grounds currently support or fail to support children's learning, play and wider development
- surveyed the existing layout and features and recorded these on a base plan
- reviewed current management policies and practice.

Stage 2: Where would we like to be?

At this stage in the process of change, you need to ask 'what would we like to be able to *do* in our grounds', not 'what would we like to be able to *have*?' Answering this question will involve thinking about:

- **Use.** How do you want to use your grounds?
- **Design.** How do the layout and features in your grounds can support their use?
- **Management.** How can you support the use and development of your grounds through management policies and practices?

Tools to help

Creating a zoning plan   What do *you* think?
Creating a vision plan   Let's talk
Creating mood boards   Using overlays
Prioritising ideas   Voting on a carousel

Use

Focusing on what *experiences* you want your pupils to have in your school grounds rather than specific features or pieces of equipment will help you avoid wasting money on changes or installations that don't really meet your needs, or prove impractical or inflexible. You may already have plenty of ideas, but don't know how to go about making the changes. Or you might want to improve the use of your outdoors but not yet know what experiences your pupils would most benefit from. You could start by considering the experiences your children have now and those that they might be missing out on not just at school but in their lives in general. One way to approach this is to look at ways in which the outdoors is special. For example, the outdoors offers opportunities for every child to experience:

- contact with nature
- getting active in different ways
- risk and challenge in a managed environment
- hands-on learning, in different areas of the curriculum
- growing, cooking and eating food
- enjoying playtimes
- socialising across different age groups and genders
- creative and cooperative play.

You might also want to consider more general outcomes, such as helping to improve:

- concentration in lessons
- pupils' sense of responsibility
- general contentment
- opportunities to engage every child with learning

- attainment
- behaviour
- motivation
- attendance rates
- opportunities for pupils to make a difference to the school
- opportunities for parents to get involved.

There are a variety of ways in which you can gather the thoughts, ideas and feelings of your pupils and staff, including preparing simple questionnaires (*Part 4: Resources – Activity 4: What do you think?*) and holding discussions and debates (*Part 4: Resources – Activity 5: Let's talk*). Through this process you will also identify issues and barriers. Make a note of them – you will have an opportunity to address them in Stage 3.

Once you have contributions from everyone you will want to put all the ideas into order. Voting activities are an effective way of getting feedback on ideas and suggestions – see *Part 4: Resources – Activity 14: Voting on a carousel*. You can also use this voting system to decide on the style of features the school likes or specific design solutions.

Once you have a rough idea of how your grounds can benefit the school, it is useful to develop this into a **vision statement**. A vision statement helps ensure everyone in the school community is heading in the same direction. Your statement may describe the type of experiences you want your children to have but could also refer to the atmosphere you wish to create, which could include the style of the space. Here is an example: 'Our school grounds will be a great place for children to play and learn in a safe and supportive environment'.

There are different ways of writing a vision statement. You could, for example:

- get those leading your project to add key words, phrases or ideas to a 'vision words' board (or the whole school could be involved). Sticky notes are ideal, but a graffiti board would work just as well. Either working as a whole group or within smaller groups, use these words and phrases to feed into the creation of a vision statement for your school grounds project.
- provide participants with a starting point for a vision statement to a help get them started. Starting points might be:
  o Our school grounds will be . . .
  o Pupils using our grounds will . . .
  o Everyone who visits our grounds will . . .

If more than one group is writing a vision statement get them to share their thoughts with the whole group; look at what is good about each statement and bring these together to form your final school grounds vision statement. Your vision statement should be available to everyone involved in the project so post it on your website, use it for funding applications but most of all make sure everyone working on the project has access to a copy. This will help keep your project on track and motivate everyone involved.

Design

Having developed your vision statement, you can start to think about how your school grounds will look and feel, and what features and resources it will contain. Even though at this stage you might only have the funds to change a small area of your grounds, a whole site approach – focusing on the overall structure right from the start – will enable you to make changes that work together in the future.

A useful first step is to create a **zoning plan**. Some of the activities that you want to take place within the grounds will conflict – for example, quiet areas do not live happily next to the football pitch! A zoning plan is an outline plan of your grounds, divided up roughly to show how different activities could take place in different areas. You don't need to be artistic to do this – and it is a good opportunity to get everyone thinking about the implications of change. You'll need to consider:

- locations for the activities you wish to take place in your grounds. It might, for example, be obvious where you should site a pond for wildlife investigations, but what about seating?
- how the inside and external spaces work together. What is access like to the outside and can this be changed? Could working or playing outside impact on what is happening inside? A space directly outside a classroom could be ideal for teaching outside but a shared courtyard space may mean that one class working outside might disturb others inside.
- how you can ensure movement around the site works successfully. Refer to previous work on desire-lines in Stage 1: Design. Pathways into and across the site will help to define how the space is divided up.
- shade and shelter – will there be places that become hot spots in the summer, or cold, windy places in the winter?
- visibility across the site – will you be creating any blind spots and does this matter?

For more information see *Part 4: Resources – Activity 10: Creating a zoning plan.*

Once you have identified the major zones and are happy with their relationship to each other and the school buildings, you can create a **vision plan** that will define your vision for the future of the school grounds. This is not a detailed plan and it may well continue to change over time. But it will define the shapes and sizes of the different spaces and existing or potential uses, users and possible improvements as well as indicating major features – for example, large areas of planting, main routes through and access points. For more information see *Part 4: Resources – Activity 11: Creating a vision plan.*

How will your grounds feel?

Thinking about the style and atmosphere of your grounds is also important. Will you, for example, be looking to create natural spaces and features? Do you want rustic or urban style of seating etc.? Mood boards are a great way of developing the sense of a place. It may also be worth incorporating references to elements, features or styles you do *not* want to feature in your grounds – for example, plastic furniture, bright colours. For more information about how to create these see *Part 4: Resources – Activity 12: Creating mood boards.*

Management

How, through management policies and practices, can you support where you would like to be in terms of the use and design of your grounds? Use the information you have collected so far, alongside the results from the *Audit* in *Part 4: Resources,* to draw up a prioritised checklist of changes needed to policies, practices and attitudes. Reviewing your management policies and practices will help ensure that everyone with responsibility for resourcing or supervising learning and play in the school grounds understands the long-term implications of physical changes. Who do you want to get involved in undertaking the overall management and everyday maintenance of your grounds? Do you want to involve pupils, parents and staff or do you want everything to be done by a contractor or caretaker/janitor? There may, for example, be a significant impact on the cost or complexity of caring for your grounds, and, if you are keen to ensure your outdoor space is, within your capacity, low maintenance, you must carefully consider what the impact of your changes will be. To help you, when considering each change/development, think about:

● replenishment
● replacement
● maintenance.

For example, if you want to install a large sandpit to encourage natural play outdoors, will the sand need to be updated or replaced regularly? How much will it cost and how often? How will you budget for this?

Sustainability

Whatever changes you make to your grounds need to be sustainable and not cost more than you can afford, either in time or money. Make sure at this stage you consider the capacity you have to manage the different aspects of your grounds; whether you are hoping to make physical change or change to the way you are using your grounds. For more help see *Part 3: Heading towards your vision – Sustainability and management.*

By the end of this stage

You will have:

● identified the types of experiences you want your pupils to have in your school grounds
● created a vision statement and a vision plan for your grounds.

All of the above constitutes the start of your **design brief**. You will be using this to communicate your plans to all users of your grounds, and later to measure your success against it. It will also, if you decide you need professional support, help external professionals – landscape architects and designers – understand your requirements.

Stage 3: How can we get there?

Once you have worked through 'Where are we now?' and 'Where would we like to be?', and identified your school's needs, you will be able to decide on design changes with the confidence that your time and money will be well spent. This stage includes:

- addressing issues and barriers
- developing detailed design ideas
- sharing your design plans.

In order for you or a designer to come up with detailed designs, either for the whole site or for specific features and areas within it, you will need to ensure you have all the information you need for a design brief (for more help with this see *Part 4: Resources – Activity 17: Developing your design brief*). If you are planning to use a designer, it is a good idea to appoint one early on in your project. They may be able to work with you on the consultation process but it may be much more cost-effective for you to do most of this yourselves, especially with the toolkit to help you! One of the advantages in appointing a designer early on is that they can let you know exactly what information they want you to collect – and you can also discuss how they would like it presented. For help in finding a designer with school grounds experience you can contact various organisations, including us (www.ltl.org.uk).

Tools to help

Prioritising ideas   Developing your design brief
Visiting other spaces for inspiration   Press release template
Life-size planning

Addressing issues and barriers

The next stage is to look at any problems you may have identified in Stage 2: 'Where would we like to be?' Some of these may be resolved by the way you manage your space; others may need design solutions. Put together as much information about what you think is needed as you can; this is especially useful if you are using a professional designer to develop the detailed solutions for you.

Some of the issues and barriers that may arise could be a result of lack of agreement. Some members of your school community, for example, may have strong views and these must be addressed to help your project progress smoothly. Everyone needs to have their views heard. This can be achieved with a suggestions box, which you could make available for comments throughout the project and/or a graffiti board on which people can add their ideas/thoughts/criticisms. If issues are raised, use the *Prioritising ideas* activity (*Part 4: Resources – Activity 13*) to decide the order in which they should be dealt with. You can then work to resolve them.

Alternatively, or in addition to, the above, you could also work in small groups to identify issues. Each group should prioritise their issues, then write these down the side of a flip chart page in order of priority. Switch sheets with another group and try to find solutions to resolve each other's issues. If you have several groups, after a few minutes, keep swapping sheets. Do this three or four times, then, with the final group or the original group, review the solutions and share with the larger group. If there are any issues that have not got satisfactory answers discuss them all together. If there are still problems park the issues for now, but ask people to think about them and respond over the following week or so. If the issue is still not resolved it may need to be accepted and the design or solutions limited because of it.

The next step is prioritising all the ideas you have gathered together. This will include the different zones or types of space in your vision plan as well as the changes you want to make to policies and practices. When you have done this you are ready to start to develop your design ideas.

Developing detailed design ideas

This is where your project starts to come alive and you can start to see how your grounds might look when you are completed. There are many different ways of developing design ideas. Do feel free to 'borrow' ideas from other environments and schools if you find something truly meets your own needs. However, be careful about choosing something just because it looks good – remember you want a solution that is right for your school and your pupils, so although an off-the-shelf feature might be easy it won't necessarily fulfil your needs.

Look at both *Part 3: Heading towards your vision* and *Part 4: Resources – Case studies* and the *More useful organisations* for inspiration and links to useful websites and sources of information. Search the internet too for ideas and visit schools and other public open spaces for inspiration (*see Part 4: Resources – Activity 15: Visiting other spaces for inspiration*). Remember to compare your needs with those of the schools featured so that you can see how their changes have made a difference. You can also look at magazines, explore what suppliers, artists, designers and craftspeople have to offer, and investigate specialists in different fields – including specialists in wildlife and biodiversity, outdoor learning, play, behaviour, sustainability, health and wellbeing, activity and sport.

Don't forget also to consider how any changes will impact on the maintenance of your grounds and the associated long-term cost implications. For example, if a pond is created, who will look after it? Will it be easier to maintain if it is closer to the buildings? Use your grounds maintenance staff as a source of advice about what will be practical. You may be surprised – not all changes will mean greater expense. For example, if you want to have a wildflower meadow you will need to mow just once or twice a year rather than every other week.

When you are deciding on design ideas there may be other issues you need to consider, such as compliance with wildlife legislation, health and safety regulations, drainage etc. There is more information about these at the end of Stage 4: Making the changes.

Here, we will look at how you might develop your own design ideas, how you can bring in experts for specific elements and how you can work with a landscape architect or other designer to develop a detailed design for some or all of your grounds.

Developing your own ideas. There may be areas of your grounds that you can design and develop yourselves – especially if you have access to specialist skills and knowledge within your school community. It is best to start by focusing on specific areas within your overall plan – such as a seating area, a performance space or a wildlife area. This can provide you with wonderful opportunities to involve pupils and the rest of the school community – asking them to draw their ideas or create models of what they would like these features of spaces to look like, remembering that you have already identified what you want to be able to *do* there before designing the solutions. They can also find images of items they have seen elsewhere that fit your brief or you can ask people to vote on a range of possible options. You can also road-test design ideas with children and adults with *Activity 16: Life-size planning* in *Part 4: Resources*. This involves participants laying out the design of an area in the space in which it is to be located to see how well it works.

Working with specialists. This might be a specialist designer, supplier or contractor – someone who has expertise in a particular area of work and who can work with your ideas to create something special for your site. Provide them with as much information as you can and think carefully about whether an off-the-shelf solution is right for you or whether you want something unique for your grounds. The latter is obviously likely to be more expensive but may be worth the extra cost as you have something that truly meets your needs and may be more aesthetically or environmentally satisfactory too.

You will find information about who can help you in *Part 4: Resources – More useful organisations*. These specialists might include:

- artists and crafts people to create murals, willow structures, sculptures or furniture that are unique for the site
- wildlife specialists who can help you develop wildlife habitats such as a meadow or pond and can help you develop a wildlife management plan for your site
- musical specialists who can help you develop instruments for your grounds
- a sustainability specialist who can work with you to look at adding features to your site such as wind turbines and solar panels
- horticultural specialists who can help you develop growing areas, sensory planting and the aesthetic aspects of your site
- a play specialist who can help you consider how you develop the way play is managed in your grounds
- play equipment manufacturers who can work with you to develop specific solutions from adventure trails to seating
- landscape architects could also be brought in to develop individual spaces, such as natural play spaces.

Working with a design professional. At this stage you may decide to use a design professional, such as a landscape architect. If you don't already have someone in mind it is a good idea to invite two or three to tender for the work. Provide them with a summary of your brief and ask for examples of previous work; photographs, the names of any schools or setting they have worked with before whom you could contact; details of their professional indemnity and public liability insurances. Invite the professionals you are interested in working with to visit. This initial visit should include a tour with small groups of pupils giving guided tours of your outdoor space. Staff, parents and pupils can all be involved in interviewing the candidates, who should be asked to discuss their general approach and initial thoughts for the commission.

Once you have appointed your design professional, they will use all the information you have gathered for your design brief to develop a detailed design plan. The more information you provide them with, the more satisfactory the outcome will be. A landscape architect or similar designer will be able to come up with detailed designs for all elements within the grounds – possibly in conjunction with other specialists, whereas specialist designers or suppliers will focus on one particular feature or area of your site. Lead them through all the work you have done; show them your survey work, your thoughts about what you would like to be able to do in your grounds as well as your vision statement, zoning plan, vision plan, mood boards, priorities and any thoughts you have about possible solutions. Don't be satisfied with off-the-shelf solutions unless they truly meet your needs. Challenge designers to be creative and don't feel afraid to question anything they come up with – after all you are the experts on how you will want to use anything new.

Ensuring joint objectives

Make sure the designer you have chosen to work with understands the process you have gone through to get your brief together. That way you will know they will be asking the right questions of you and themselves as they develop their design ideas. Bear in mind also that the designer is likely to focus on landscape objectives while you will be focusing on educational objectives.

Landscape objectives might include:

- providing a safe, diverse and stimulating environment
- building in flexibility to accommodate change/development
- balancing design, management and use against aesthetic, function and financial considerations
- incorporating sustainability within the design – for example surface water treatment.

Educational objectives might include:

- providing outdoor teaching spaces that are sheltered, safe and secure
- stimulating creativity and curiosity in learning
- providing opportunities for enriching the curriculum
- providing opportunities for creative and active play.

Landscape and educational objectives both need to be met, and should be considered within the briefing process so that both the designer and the school understand the perspective of each other and ask appropriate questions.

Sharing your design ideas

Once you have your design ideas make sure you display them prominently, together with your school development plan. Provide opportunities for everyone to make comments, either by adding notes to the plan (sticky notes are good for this), or through discussion during lessons. It is important to check that all members of staff – especially those with responsibility for maintaining the grounds – are aware of your proposed changes. You should also publicise your plans as widely as possible; at the very least through your parents' newsletter but this is also a good opportunity to get local media attention. Emphasise in your press release (see *Part 4: Resources – Activity 18: Press release template*) how the plans have been developed with the pupils' involvement and how they will improve the school. And don't be shy about asking for help, you never know who might be reading.

By the end of this stage

You should have:

- worked to resolve outstanding issues
- decided upon key elements of your grounds
- developed detailed designs for specific features
- had input from the whole school community.

Stage 4: Making the changes

Once you have a developed and costed your design ideas for your outdoor space, it's time to start making the changes. This involves:

- creating an action plan
- deciding who will do the work
- creating a management plan
- celebrating
- reflecting . . . where are we now?

Tools to help

Skills survey
Bag gardens
Building a shelter
Building homes for minibeasts

Constructing a rainwater collection system
Healthy?
Ten steps to running a great activity

Creating an action plan

An action plan, whether in the form of a basic calendar or a more detailed document, will help make sure all your tasks are completed and everyone knows who is responsible for what. Depending on the scale of your development you may or may not have the time or money to make all the changes at once (see the *Quick wins* box on page 32 for quick and cheap changes).

This should include information about:

- the changes you wish to make
- their place in school policy – for example, a management plan
- schemes of work, play and environmental policies, health and safety, insurance etc.
- a breakdown of the project into manageable tasks
- who is taking responsibility for which part of the project, taking into account expertise and availability
- a timeline showing when the changes will happen – some changes will be seasonal, others you may wish to do in term-time or when the school is on holiday
- how the space being developed will be used
- what it adds to the learning and or play experiences of the pupils
- how the changes will be resourced
- how much they will cost
- who is to undertake the work.

Quick wins

Some changes to school grounds can be made more quickly and cheaply than others. The value of doing these first is to increase motivation, and offer pupils in their final year a chance to have an impact on their grounds. These changes include:

- enhancing planting
- adding moveable planters
- bringing in loose play equipment that can be lent out at playtimes – whether 'off the shelf' or materials to support natural play, such as circles of wood, sticks, large stones or sheets for den building
- creating and installing art works
- changing mowing regimes to create long grass areas
- developing existing unused or underused spaces
- developing schemes of work so the outside is used more for teaching and learning
- developing a play strategy
- creating wildlife habitats such as minibeast hotels or bird boxes.

Remember that any quick changes you make must allow for any future changes to your grounds, so ideas that do not include permanent physical changes will be the best for now.

More lessons outdoors?

As part of the audit you will have looked at how much teaching you take outside. From this you may decide to take a look at how to increase the level of teaching outside. Part of this process should include looking at current schemes of work and lesson plans. When you are deciding upon your schemes of work for the term or year to come, review which elements could be taken outside. Work in groups or individually to consider what you might do outside. This might include lots of short elements as well as whole lessons or even themed days or weeks. Activities in your school grounds may also help you prepare for and follow up on visits to other sites.

Your aim should be to have ideas for going outside scattered through schemes of work, so that you can be flexible about when to go outside, to make the most of weather etc. Share your ideas with colleagues and consider team teaching if you do not feel totally confident about taking ideas out on your own. More information about how to develop your teaching practice is available from Learning through Landscapes (www.ltl.org.uk).

Deciding who will do the practical work

There are many different jobs that will need doing if you are making physical changes to your grounds. Some of these will need specialists to undertake the work, either on their own or with help from the school, while others could be completed by members of the school community, including pupils.

Pupils. There will be plenty of tasks that the pupils themselves can get involved in – such as planting or painting, making art works or helping to create more complex features alongside a specialist. Even when it is not appropriate for pupils to carry out work themselves they can still be involved – watching work in progress, recording what happens with a diary/photographs or video, or hearing about the project from the contractors in an assembly.

It is important that whoever is leading the work has a clear understanding of what is to be done, and it may be necessary to bring in an external organisation to help you – such as a wildlife or horticultural specialist if you are undertaking planting. However, you may also have the necessary skills within your school community to run some projects so your skills audit (*Part 4: Resources*) will be invaluable in finding out who can help with which projects.

Staff, parents and other volunteers. A school grounds project can be an excellent way of encouraging parents and other members of the school community to come into school. Parents who have practical skills, such as building, carpentry, gardening or painting, may also be the same people who find it difficult to come into school to help with reading and other 'academic' tasks. Your skills audit (*Part 4: Resources*) will not only find out what people have expertise in but also what they are willing to help with given some support. Willing pairs of hands can be particularly useful as long as you have someone who can lead on the work on the ground, so do check that whoever is in charge knows what they are doing! You should also check out that you have appropriate insurance to cover those undertaking the work as well as its use when it has been completed. Health and safety are obviously very important considerations and a risk assessment/risk-benefit analysis should be carried out both of the work itself and whatever feature is made as a result. Working parties are a great way of getting people involved – and personal invitation is always the best way to get people involved, rather than a general invite which can easily be ignored or thought to be 'not about me'. To add to the draw of this type of event why not add in hot soup or even a barbecue so those people who are willing to serve the refreshments will be as important as those undertaking the work on the ground.

Professional designers. Landscape architects can help you design and implement both large-scale and smaller projects. They can make a valuable contribution to your plans, bringing creative thinking as well as broad experience to the use and arrangement of your outdoor space. They can help you develop an overall concept and strategy for longer-term developments and turn your strategic vision into reality by preparing detailed designs, contract documentation and getting work implemented on site. They will also have knowledge of any planning, health and safety or insurance requirements as well as contractual requirements – either between you and the designer or a contractor undertaking the work on the ground. You can choose to work with a landscape architect right from the start or bring them in once you have identified and prioritised your needs or want more help with detailed designs. One good reason for getting them involved early on is that they can let you know what information they would like you to gather and any format that they would like to receive this in. Some landscape architects will be experienced in pupil consultation but many will not, and if you can do much of this yourselves it will also make your money go further. Garden designers or other specialist designers and artists can help you create detailed designs for defined areas or features within your grounds. They will bring expert knowledge about their particular area of specialism and most will wish to focus on their particular skills and knowledge rather than look at the whole site. Those who are LTL accredited can help you look at your overall plans. However, do make sure that any work does fit into an overall plan as described throughout this toolkit.

Contractors and suppliers. This includes quite a wide mix of expertise from playground equipment designers and suppliers to fencers, wallers, painters and horticulturalists. As with anyone you are working with make sure they have the knowledge and skills to undertake the work and that they fully understand what you want. Suppliers' catalogues can be a great place for inspiration but you don't have to stop there.

See if a contractor is able to work with your children, whether through active involvement or watching what is being done. Make sure they have all the health and safety and insurance requirements you need for them to work on site and insist on a high quality of finish and clearing up of the site once they have completed the work. With landscape work you will also want to consider a clause in their contract that insures they replant any plant losses in the first year of growth and undertake appropriate maintenance. Work with whoever undertakes your usual maintenance too to make sure you are not double-booking the work on site, or that each of those involved thinks it is someone else's job to do something so that no one completes a given task. If you are working with a landscape architect they will be able to help you with this type of contract issue. And don't forget, if you are removing spoil you may be able to reuse it elsewhere to create mounds and hillocks.

Skills audit: Finding volunteers

Asking members of your school community to volunteer help with specific tasks needed to make changes not only means you get help for free, but also encourages everyone on board. First, however, you will need to find out what skills everybody has. Think about what you need doing, and what skills this requires. Some tasks will need specialist knowledge and skills, others will just need enthusiasm. Some skills may not be obvious – such as tea maker – but can be really important to keep people happy on a working day.

Draw up a list of these different tasks – use images demonstrating the ideas as well as text to make it accessible to all – and provide a space on the form for everyone to put the level of their skill. Leave space also for anyone with skills you hadn't thought of to add their name. Volunteers that you might need could include:

- designer
- minute taker/secretary
- artist/craftsperson
- bricklayer
- painter and decorator
- tea maker
- childminder
- form filler
- accountant/bookkeeper
- gardener.

Creating a management plan

A carefully thought out and regularly updated management plan will help direct the development of your grounds and ensure the space remains usable all year round and into the future. If you already have a grounds or garden maintenance contract, speak to your contractor about your planned changes. They may be able to help implement the changes themselves. Alternatively, you may have a caretaker or gardener who can be involved.

A management plan should include details of:

- the aims and objectives of the management of your site – this might include your vision statement but could also be more specific, such as to encourage more birds into your grounds; to teach more lessons around the pond
- what needs doing – the specific maintenance requirements of each element in the grounds
- who will carry out the work
- the frequency of work to be carried out, including specific times of year that it needs to be done.

It can be really useful for the management plan to include a visual representation of the grounds. Use a plan of your site marking on it the different elements that require specific management, and display the timetable of work to be done and by whom. This can be set out as a calendar using a key to identify tasks and who has responsibility for what, who is doing what work when.

From this you can write a document that gives you more detail as to what is required from each task throughout the year. This is the type of information that will need to be included in any maintenance contract you have for the site, but it will also be useful if the school community itself is to undertake any of the maintenance tasks.

Celebrating . . .

Making changes to school grounds takes a lot of thought, hard work, consultation, engagement and commitment. It is important to take every opportunity to celebrate achievements and remember why you are doing it.

- **Celebrate with the pupils.** By involving the children in your project you'll have a wealth of material to use: pictures they have drawn, photos they have taken, questions they have asked. Turn them into books and displays so that the children, parents and staff can enjoy them and look back on things together.
- **Celebrate with the parents and the wider community.** An outdoor fête, festival or summer party can be a great way to involve parents and the local community in celebrating the changes you have made and what you do outdoors in your school. Encourage adults to remember and pass on the games they played as a child. Use the occasion to encourage parents to share different skills, such as cooking or making music outdoors. You can go on celebrating outdoors throughout the year and linking to a wide range of different cultures, festivals and traditions.
- **Celebrate with the staff.** Staff engagement is essential in making an outdoor project successful. Recognise this by supporting them with professional development opportunities. Encourage them to undertake action research about the impact of any changes and/or rerun the *Audit*. Give them opportunities to share what they have learned and any changes in practice with other staff.

- **Let others learn from what you have done.** Use the media to tell your story and write up your experience for a case study. LTL is always interested to hear your story, however small the changes you have made. We would love to see your photos or children's work. With your permission we can use your case study to inspire others across the UK and beyond.

And reflecting . . . Where are we now?

Once you have been through the process you will want and need to evaluate what you have done. Does it do what you set out to do or have there been outcomes you didn't expect? – these might be good or bad! The outcomes of your evaluation will feed into what you do next – so that you can start to move through the process once more and decide on what your next project is going to be.

Look back at your original vision, aims and objectives, You may also use video, photographic images and observation – just as you did when you were getting this project started. Using the same techniques can mean it is easier to compare the changes. Reuse Section 1 of the audit too for the elements that you made changes to and compare the results. Use the information from the audit to decide what you are going to focus on next.

It is likely that the changes will have an impact on more than one of the areas below, but we have separated them out to help you identify specific elements of your project.

Use. If you are taking more aspects outside can you compare your results after this approach to those before you went outdoors? Much of this information you will already be gathering but some might need new tools such as pupil and staff questionnaires and interviews. Issues you might want to consider could include:

- attainment – compare one year group as they move up through the school and also the same year level before and after the change, e.g. look at your Year 6 results for pupils who have not done much work outside and compare with Year 6 pupils who have
- behaviour – if possible look at measuring positive behaviour, not just negative
- attendance – your changes could make a difference to how much children enjoy their time at school and, for some, this may lower their absenteeism
- motivation – more difficult to assess but a simple pupil questionnaire could help you see if children are enjoying their lessons or play more when they are taken outside
- accident records – depending on what you do you may find accident numbers go up, but the severity of them goes down.

Design. Again your aim is to find out what worked well and what didn't. To a certain extent, the success of the design will become apparent depending on how much the grounds are used, and how easy etc. they are to manage. Other issues to look at, however, which may inform how you progress with the next stage of your development should include:

- Did the costs stay within budget? If not why not?
- Did you work well with your designer?
  - o   Did they understand your needs and interpret them in the design successfully?
  - o   Did they work well with pupils, staff and other adults?
  - o   Were they able to fully engage with the school?
  - o   Did they present their ideas well so that you could understand them?

- Did the finished result end up as you expected? If not, what was different about it and can you explain why?
- Does the design work well in the site?
  - o Does it look and feel right in the site?
  - o Does it do what you wanted? – more wildlife, more positive play, more lessons outside?
  - o Does it solve any specific problems such as access, waterlogging or shade?
  - o Can you use the rest of the site easily as well as this new feature or space?
  - o Are spaces accessible and able to be supervised sufficiently?
  - o Is the site, and individual features within it, safe?
  - o Does the design allow for changes in use and design over time?
  - o Can the design be used in a flexible way and will it allow for change in the future?
  - o Can you use it for a wide range of activities?
  - o Were the materials used sustainable? Maybe you even recycled materials from your grounds.
  - o Did you use local specialists to help implement the design?
- Talk to parents about the changes, what do they think and what do their children tell them?
- Ask pupils and staff, both teaching and non-teaching, about how they feel about the changes in the way they use the grounds.

Management. Don't leave it too long to see if management and maintenance is working! The longer you leave it the harder it will be to put right. If you have all your systems in place and know what you are trying to achieve then making sure this is happening should be straightforward.

- If you are keeping records for the use of the grounds, you will know if this has increased.
- Interview the staff – teaching and non-teaching – to see how they find managing pupils outside, whether for lessons or playtimes. Have the changes made a difference? If so how? Do further changes need to be made?
- Keep reviewing your management plan – some things will need to be changed each year – to make sure it still fits in with your needs.

Legislation and policies

If you are undertaking small projects it is unlikely that you will need to worry about many of these areas listed below. However, it is worth checking through the list just in case there is something you need to act upon. If you are working with a landscape architect they should be aware of these issues but do check with them if you are unsure. Legislation may vary between England, Scotland, Wales and Northern Ireland, so check with your local authority to be sure.

Biodiversity. There will be someone within your local authority who can guide you on national and local policy. Some species that might be found in your grounds have special protection which means you need to be careful about not destroying their habitats or disturbing them. They will have different levels of protection, including European legislation and UK protection. Amongst the list of key species are:

- bats
- great crested newts
- dormice
- otters
- badgers
- birds
- widespread reptiles
- water voles
- white-clawed crayfish
- hedgehogs
- invertebrates
- stag beetles.

There will be people within your local Wildlife Trust, The Conservation Volunteers or local authority who have the knowledge, skills or licences required to help you with this aspect of your grounds. This will include information on your local Biodiversity Action Plan (BAP) which links to the UK BAP and this will include guidance and information for schools.

Trees. Some schools may have Tree Preservation Orders (TPO) on their trees or be in a conservation area. In either case you will need permission from your local authority to cut these down or carry out other work on them.

Contractors carrying out work on your site will also need to take care of existing trees so that they are not damaged when work is being carried out on site. They should identify a tree protection zone and erect fencing to form an exclusion zone if there is any risk of damage.

You should also make sure your trees are safe by having them regularly inspected. The duty of care is on the landowner.

Planning permission and building regulations. Many changes to your grounds will not require planning permission. However, there are some projects where it will be necessary to apply for permission. A useful website to help you find out is www.planningportal.gov.uk/permission/ but your local authority planning officers should be able to advise you too. Features that might need planning permission include fences, wind turbines and solar panels.

Construction, design and management regulations. You must notify the Health and Safety Executive of the site if the construction work is expected to either:

- last longer than 30 days; or
- involve more than 500 person days of construction work.

These are likely to be projects where you have a designer on board and they should take responsibility for fulfilling the requirements of these regulations.

Part 3: Heading towards your vision

This part of the toolkit looks at specific themes that schools often find are their priorities for development. Once you have completed the *Audit* and seen where your strengths and weaknesses lie you may well have found this is the case for you.

It is really important to maintain a whole-site approach to your grounds developments so when using this section:

- **Do** so *after* completing the *Audit* – this is the first stage in your development and will help you as you move through process of change for your grounds.
- **Don't** get too bogged down with specific ideas too early on – keep an open mind, you may well discover that one solution actually helps you resolve a completely different issue too.
- **Do** create your vision statement and vision plan so that you know where you are heading overall.
- **Do** then focus in on specific aspects and areas as highlighted in your audit, in your plans and in your prioritisation. This is where this section of the toolkit will be most useful.

Under each key theme below you will find information and research about why this aspect of your grounds is important. You will then find ideas on how to make this work in practice – building on the experience of hundreds of schools, we have put together some key ideas for how to go about making the change for each themed area. There are also some top tips to help you on your way. Finally, we have provided you with information about organisations that can help you for each of the themes.

Use this information in combination with the case studies (one on each theme), the images and resources in *Part 4* to help you come up with ideas and solutions that are right for you. The information here is intended to inspire you and challenge your ideas about what can be done so don't just copy what you've seen elsewhere, be creative and make your school grounds the best they can be.

Teaching and learning

Learning experiences outside the classroom are often the most memorable lessons, helping children to make sense of the world around them, and allowing them to gain knowledge and confidence that they can transfer back to the classroom. There are opportunities here that don't exist indoors, and simply having more space allows a more physical, experiential way of learning which suits many children. Young children in particular need physical movement as part of their learning. Noisy, messy activities are easier and the outdoors provides more sensory stimulation, making learning a whole-body experience. Relationships outside the classroom are different too: children report that their teachers seem friendlier and the lessons more interesting.

Children don't simply learn more, or learn better, when freed from their desks. They also learn differently, experiencing improvements in four specific ways:

- Cognitive impacts – concerning knowledge, understanding and other academic outcomes
- Affective impacts – encompassing attitudes, values, beliefs and self-perceptions
- Interpersonal/social impacts – including communication skills, leadership and teamwork
- Physical/behavioural impacts – relating to physical fitness, physical skills, personal behaviours and social actions.

Dillon et al. (2005: 26)

How to make it work

Think about how to make your space rich in experiences (weather vane, signposts, ponds, sundial, art work, standard measures marked out etc.) – you would not expect your classroom to be barren so why would you expect the playground to be? A lot of learning can happen in a space that encourages curiosity and exploration. Think ahead too: if you want to install a pond imagine what you'll need to hold lessons alongside: a dipping area, a nearby space to gather and chat in small groups or as a class, and storage for equipment.

But don't be restricted to areas specifically designed to support the curriculum – get to know your outside spaces and think about the learning potential they offer: quiet, contemplative spaces for writing poetry, reading stories etc.; wide open spaces for activities such as making and flying kites or playing human battleships; researching the wildlife and/or edible offerings of a hedgerow; investigating organic approaches to gardening to promote healthy eating or support science; finding out about how to manage a piece of woodland for play and conservation. Think too about using the maintenance of your outdoor space as a learning tool rather than leaving it to one person or specific group.

Sometimes it's also worth changing what you are studying to fit in with the outdoors (for example, investigate measuring when your plants are ready to harvest and cook).

Designing in spaces to gather and shelter near to where you want to take teaching is vital but having suitable clothing available for the whole class will also help you to access the grounds whatever the weather (and don't forget that the changing seasons – and changing weather patterns – are great topics for investigation too).

Keep an open mind – see the potential in all resources and have the confidence in your own risk assessments and/or risk-benefit analysis to give life to old objects. School grounds developments do not happen overnight and if you are open to the possibilities of donated objects you can create a magical and bespoke area.

TOP TIPS

- Don't see going outside as an 'extra' – look at what you have to teach and work out how to teach it outside or as part of your development project.
- Go through you existing schemes of work – how can you make them come alive outdoors?
- Activities outside don't have to last a whole lesson. Start small, collecting data and bringing it into a lesson, then build time spent outside as you build confidence.

Your grounds are also an ideal place to plan for and follow up on learning outside the classroom trips. Using your grounds to introduce topics gets children interested from the beginning. Following up your trip with activities in your grounds will also help you embed the learning gained from your trip.

Useful organisations

The Council for Learning Outside the Classroom – www.lotc.org.uk
Department for Education (England) – www.education.gov.uk
Department for Education (Northern Ireland) – www.deni.gov.uk
Education Scotland – www.educationscotland.gov.uk
Education Wales – www.learning.wales.gov.uk
Learning through Landscapes – www.ltl.org.uk

A feature added by one generation for a future generation to benefit from.

Not all features need be permanent – this river was a temporary addition that provided for a wide range of focused lesson activities.

Not every lesson requires physical change – lessons can still be innovative and creative like this writing with chalk on paving.

The process of planning changes to your grounds can open up curriculum opportunities. Here pupils plant 'flowers' to show where they'd like to have real flowers.

Specific features like this newly created air raid shelter opens up many opportunities for making learning come alive.

Here one lesson activity led to the creation of a resource for future lessons – the names of those who created these giraffes are also displayed for all to see.

Considering the type of features that are added to a site can provide new learning opportunities – here a basalt rock creates opportunities for the study of geology and geometric shapes as well as marking the edge to a pond.

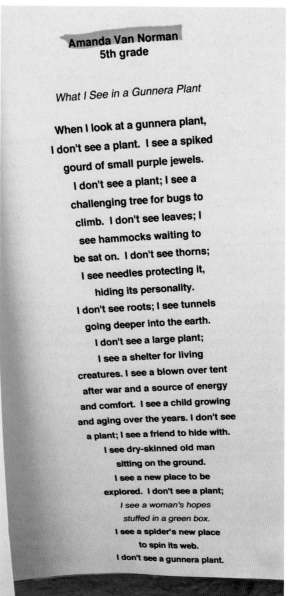

Amanda Van Norman
5th grade

What I See in a Gunnera Plant

When I look at a gunnera plant,
I don't see a plant. I see a spiked
gourd of small purple jewels.
I don't see a plant; I see a
challenging tree for bugs to
climb. I don't see leaves; I
see hammocks waiting to
be sat on. I don't see thorns;
I see needles protecting it,
hiding its personality.
I don't see roots; I see tunnels
going deeper into the earth.
I don't see a large plant;
I see a shelter for living
creatures. I see a blown over tent
after war and a source of energy
and comfort. I see a child growing
and aging over the years. I don't see
a plant; I see a friend to hide with.
I see dry-skinned old man
sitting on the ground.
I see a new place to be
explored. I don't see a plant;
I see a woman's hopes
stuffed in a green box.
I see a spider's new place
to spin its web.
I don't see a gunnera plant.

This poem is the result of creative writing based around the development of the school's grounds. Could this have been written if the pupil had not seen the gunnera in real life?

Here features are incorporated into the grounds that pupils can learn from every day – water is collected from the roof of a straw bale building and a wormery is used for creating compost.

Play

All children should be able to play – to engage in freely chosen, personally directed, intrinsically motivated behaviour that actively engages the child. In his blog *Freedom to Learn* (June 2012) published on the website www.psychologytoday.com, research professor of psychology at Boston College, Peter Gray, explains why free play is so important to children: 'In play, children practice many skills that are crucial for healthy development. They practice physical and manual skills, intellectual skills, and social skills . . . They also practice emotional skills. In play, children learn how to regulate their fear and anger and thereby how to maintain emotional control in threatening real-life situations.'

There is also growing research that suggests that children can be more active at playtime than during their PE lessons and that the way that school grounds are developed and resourced can have a significant impact on the level of activity that takes place there.

The natural play space encourages children to use different muscle groups. In addition, compared with the baseline study, there was evidence of an increase in the accumulated number of steps and in the minutes of physical activity across all year groups for both boys and girls over the school day. The increase is equivalent to 10% of their daily recommended minutes and steps.

Groves (2011: 3)

How to make it work

Children need to have a variety of play options available to them so that they are provided with opportunities to be active and challenged, creative and social, to make their own choices and develop their independence.

Play comes in a wide variety of forms and no two schools will have the same solutions but there are some key principles and ideas that you can follow that will help you make playtime in your grounds a positive experience for all.

Providing a range of loose equipment is a quick and effective starting point. Consider the variety of equipment that you provide – many schools will provide ropes, hoops, balls and other standard play equipment but why not include materials from a 'scrap store' such as crates, inner tubes from carpet rolls, boxes etc. or more natural materials such as wooden discs, branches, straw bales and cloth to make dens from.

Creating a more varied landscape can also encourage more types of play. Think about the range of experiences you want your children to have – maybe experiences they are not getting at home. Provide opportunities for children to explore, get wet, build dens and hide. These are all relatively simple experiences to provide for but they may require a shift in thinking regarding play provision, requiring all staff to identify the opportunities they want to create for children, how these can be achieved and how your shared vision will be communicated with parents. They also need to understand that taking risks, in a safe environment, is necessary for children's development, helping them assess risk and danger in different situations. Use a risk-benefit approach to look at how the positives of different features can be weighed up against their risks.

Writing a simple play policy that identifies the benefits of play can have a number of advantages including the development of a common understanding of the role of play, a practical working tool for developing and improving the play environment and an induction document for new staff. Share the benefits of play with parents, engage children and start slowly – for example, trialling access to an area or the introduction of specific resources. Reassure anxious parents through involvement, the promotion of what you are trying to achieve and by sharing your risk-benefit assessment approach.

TOP TIPS

- Get parents on board by inviting them to play sessions where the children are using loose materials.
- Agree on the role of the adult in promoting free play – keep adult supervision to a minimum and allow play to be child led.
- Work with children to agree a behaviour code – for example, looking out for each other, use of indoor/outdoor shoes, identifying the height to which children can climb trees etc.

Useful organisations

Learning through Landscapes – www.ltl.org.uk (search 'natural play'; also
    www.youtube.com/schoolgroundsuk)
Free Play Network – www.freeplaynetwork.org.uk
Playboard Northern Ireland – www.playboard.org
Playlink – www.playlink.org
Play England – www.playengland.org.uk
Play Scotland – www.playscotland.org
Play Wales – www.playwales.org.uk

These boys are making the most of a woodland area to develop their imaginations through natural play.

Photograph: © Malcolm Cochrane.

Providing a range of loose equipment and encouraging natural play enables these pupils, and member of staff, to travel around the world through their play.

Photograph: © Malcolm Cochrane.

Large elements of play equipment are just one part of the play provision within this school's grounds.

These sculptural elements provide the school with a unique feature that also enables children to test their limits and take risks within a safe environment.

Providing sand and water can support children's imaginative play – think about how children of all ages enjoy playing on the beach, building dens, making structures and inventing games.

Simple climbing holds create a traversing wall, low to the ground yet challenging all pupils from the most athletic to those who find physical activity more difficult.

Storage of loose equipment in simple bays allows children to access it easily for play and put things away at the end of a session.

These boys are using a selection of loose equipment to find a space in the grounds to create a den.

The hidden curriculum

When we talk about the hidden curriculum of school grounds we are talking about the messages and meaning that everyone, and particularly your pupils, read from the outdoor spaces around them. So if the grounds are dull and uncared for the children read this as being a space that is not important and, as it is space designed for them, it impacts on how they feel and behave in that space too.

Research by Learning through Landscapes (1994: 64) found that: 'Children's attitude and behaviour are determined to a considerable extent, by the design of school grounds.'

We also know this ourselves – we feel better, happier and more comfortable if we are in spaces that are pleasant to be in, and feel uneasy if our surroundings are dreary or in a state of disrepair. So is it any wonder children react to an environment they spend so much time in every day?

How to make it work

If children are affected so much by school grounds it tells us that it is important to get the design of those grounds right. So consider both the overall feel of your site as it is now and also different spaces within it. You may find that pupils naturally avoid some parts of your grounds and this may well be because of how they feel when they are in these spaces.

As part of the process of developing your grounds you will be thinking about your vision for your grounds and the ethos of your school and how this can be reflected in your site. The messages you want to convey in your grounds will be reflected by how you develop them, and this could be different for different areas as well as finding a 'style' or feeling for your grounds as a whole.

Ask yourself how you want your children to feel in your grounds. You may want them to feel safe, to feel valued and to be confident outside. You may want to show to everyone who uses the site that certain things are important to you – creativity, a sense of place, local heritage, culture or faith. You may also want to show that sustainability is important to you or that you love wildlife or gardening.

Every element you add to your grounds can help to develop this sense of place. Whether you choose seating made from natural materials or use more high-tech solutions, whether you display pupil's art work in your grounds or have worked with an artist to create a welcoming entrance – all these elements will reveal something about your school.

You may also think about creating different atmospheres in different spaces. Maybe you want some quiet, secluded, intimate spaces where flowers and shrubs produce not only an aesthetically pleasing environment but also one that has a range of wonderful aromas. Or maybe you would like some large, open spaces that are perfect for performances, or include natural features ideal for creative play.

TOP TIPS

- Ask pupils what their favourite places are – or visit some diverse places that feel different. What makes them special? Use some of these elements in the design of your special spaces.

- Think about colour. This can have a huge impact on how people feel – do some research to find out what colours are best for the different types of space you are wishing to create.
- Make sure that everything you add to the outside gets as much care and attention as things added to the inside.

Useful organisations

Arts Council – www.artscouncil.org.uk
Arts Council Northern Ireland – www.artscouncil-ni.org
Arts Wales – www.artswales.org.uk
Common Ground – www.commonground.org.uk
Learning through Landscapes – www.ltl.org.uk
Scottish Arts – www.scottisharts.org.uk

It is clear that play is given a high priority in this school's grounds.

Photograph: © Malcolm Cochrane.

This totem pole has been designed to reflect the natural environment and wildlife that is found in the school's local area.

This mosaic sends messages that different faiths are respected within this school community.

Using numbers to decorate the fence show that learning takes place outside as well as in.

A welcoming sign using a multitude of faces, national dress and language tells visitors that all are welcome in this school.

This gate sends the message that you will find something special as you pass through it.

This well-worn bench sends out many messages about how the outdoors is viewed and valued. This was one of the very few features in the grounds before the school developed their site.

"If children are going to care for the earth, then working and playing with the very stuff of existence is a priority."

David Hawkins

A notice emphasises the value this school puts on the natural world and leaves all visitors with an understanding of their priorities and beliefs.

Health and wellbeing

Time spent outdoors is vital for children's physical and mental health and wellbeing. The drive to get children more physically active is a national concern – and as active children are more likely to be active adults, it is important to find different ways of encouraging activity at school, especially as more and more children are becoming less and less active at home.

School grounds have always been designed to encourage activity, but mainly through formal sports provision and not all your pupils will be sports enthusiasts. For them, as well as the sports fans, playtime is a vitally important time to get them active. Playtime also offers children the chance to experience risk and challenge in a supervised situation, helping them develop essential life skills, whether it is climbing, jumping or balancing or understanding the importance of having access to shade.

School grounds are not just places that encourage good physical activity, they are also excellent places to help children learn about healthy food. Here they can grow their own crops and cook their own meals.

And as more children spend less time outside, the impact on their mental health is becoming a concern. Access to the natural world is vital for mental health – and school grounds can allow children to have daily contact with plants, wildlife and the changing seasons. Tim Gill makes a clear argument that 'spending time in nearby nature leads to improvements in mental health and emotional regulation, both for specific groups of children (such as those with ADHD) and for children as a whole' (2011: 8).

How to make it work

The design and management of school grounds can have a large impact on how they support health and wellbeing. Play areas, for example, can be created and managed to support different types of physical activity, for individuals as well as for small or large groups. Simply providing more games equipment at playtimes can increase physical activity, while loose equipment such as hoops, skipping ropes, large sticks and ropes all inspire exercise, and playground markings can promote running and jumping games. Just as important is how you manage playtimes to encourage all children to take part in activities – so training your supervising staff is essential to positive, active playtimes. The layout and design of your grounds will also have a big effect on the character and use of the spaces – challenging equipment and features will help children learn about risk taking, testing their physical abilities in a safe environment. For more guidance on developing your space for active play see *Part 3: Heading towards your vision – Play* (page 43).

Taking lessons outside also helps to increase the general level of activity, while working in the school garden, for example, can instil a love growing that can continue to help keep children active throughout their lives. For more guidance on developing your space for growing see *Part 3: Heading towards your vision – Growing* (page 60).

TOP TIPS

- Think about the all-round health of your pupils and how features and elements can contribute to the different aspects of their health.
- Consider the needs of all your pupils so that one group's play requirements don't take over the space every day, and every child has options for different types of activity each day.
- Plan for the long term as well as the short term – consider, for example, planting trees to create shade while using temporary shade in form of awnings, shade sails or just sheets and tarpaulins hung around the site in the meantime.

Useful organisations

Healthy Living in Scotland – http://www.scotland.gov.uk/Topics/Education/Schools/HLivi/
Healthy Schools in England – http://www.education.gov.uk/schools/pupil support/pastoralcare/a0075278/healthy-schools
Healthy Schools Northern Ireland – http://www.healthpromotionagency.org.uk/work/hpschools/menu.htm
Learning through Landscapes – www.ltl.org.uk
Royal Society for Prevention of Accidents – www.rospa.com
Welsh Network of Healthy Schools Schemes – http://wales.gov.uk/topics/health/improvement/schools/schemes/?lang=en

Think about how features outside might be used in different ways by pupils and whether this is going to be safe – as these seats are.

Photograph: © Malcolm Cochrane.

Pupils enjoy the freedom of being outside even when it is raining.

Photograph: © Malcolm Cochrane.

It is important to weigh up the benefits and risks of activities in deciding where the limits of acceptable behaviour will be for your pupils.

Photograph: © Malcolm Cochrane.

Make sure that children get outside throughout the year, even when the snows come.

Small play equipment can help to encourage active play.

Incorporating risk and challenge into the school grounds is important for pupils to stretch themselves and find out where their limits lie whilst within a safe environment.

Growing fruit and vegetables in the school's grounds may encourage pupils to try eating a greater variety of healthy food.

Shade is often lacking in many schools and planting trees is something that not only creates more shade but also brings natural features into the grounds.

Access and inclusion

Inclusive play is not merely about inclusion: carefully considered outdoor spaces can offer opportunities for children across a whole range of abilities.

> Equally important is the provision of high-quality play opportunities to children regardless of their needs and abilities. While children won't always be able to participate in *all* activities, an inclusive project should offer *all* children a real choice of play activities.
>
> (Ludvigsen *et al.* 2005: 3)

Access for all pupils into your site from inside and around your site needs to be considered, this does not mean there should be no challenges along the pathways – and pupils with different needs will find some routes more difficult to access than others, so consider different surfaces, signage, slopes and steps, access and exit points as well as passing and resting places along the way.

How to make it work

Children with additional special needs often have a number of people working with them – teachers, teaching assistants, pastoral care, parents etc. – and during your school grounds development you will want to ensure that everyone is on board. People will often have different views, for example, on how much risk is acceptable, so identifying your needs as a school and developing a shared vision for your outside space is vital. From a design point of view, some key areas to consider will include ensuring you are providing opportunities for:

● **Movement and challenge.** All children need to be challenged, some more than others. Aim for a variety of activity such as climbing, sliding, rolling, swinging, throwing, balancing etc. Consider adaptations to existing equipment (graded options on equipment/hills, a handrail to mark edges, grills to look through bridges etc.).

- **A place to rest.** Playtime can be overpowering – areas of less hectic activity can reduce sensory overload from noise (wind/other children), the glare of the sun and at the same time provide spaces to hide/watch others.
- **Role play.** 'Real' activities such as filling plant pots, sweeping leaves and watering plants can provide for children who find it hard to improvise.
- **Sharing.** This ensures some areas are not seen as being 'special' or 'different'– for example, table-top sand can be adjacent and connected to low-level sand with sand hoists, funnels, conveyors; spaces for parents, carers and friends can be provided on swings, slides, bouncers, paths etc.
- **Sensory experiences.** Children with altered perceptions may see the world in different ways or have a preference for/against textures/smells/colours. Consider how water, light (shadows and colours), planting (texture, fragrance, shape etc.), sound can affect a space. Include features such as sand, mud and water that can be manipulated/ felt by hands/feet/whole body.
- **Natural play.** Loose parts – from logs and tyres to collections of natural materials (branches, leaves, stones, shells, pebbles, seed heads etc.) – add a valuable and cost-effective dimension to play, not only fostering inventiveness, discovery and creativity but also helping everyone share, interact and play more actively than with fixed equipment.
- **Journeys.** Choices of routes around a site offer play opportunities and decision-making options for all children, helping them to develop autonomy and confidence. Ensure routes, entrances and arrival points are clear; use landmarks and texture changes to help children orientate themselves.
- **Comfort and safety.** This includes places to sit – in groups and individually – and places that offer shade and shelter. A range of seating can help meet a variety of needs; similarly shade and shelter – which is important for all users, including staff, parents and carers – should meet a wide range of needs, including intimate spaces, group activities, one-to-one and retreat.

TOP TIPS

- Consider the access from inside your buildings to your outside spaces as well as access routes around your site.
- Use different surfaces in different parts of the grounds so that pupils gain a range of experiences from just travelling around your site.
- As well as play, consider how pupils with different disabilities will be able to access *learning* outside. Think about routes around the site, seating provision, space within a seating area for wheelchairs, clear signage and acoustics.

Useful publications and organisations

Naturally Inclusive by Laura Browning and Felicity Robinson – design and training guide published by Learning through Landscapes (2011)
Sense Scotland – www.sensescotland.org.uk
The Sensory Trust – www.sensorytrust.org.uk
Thrive – www.thrive.org.uk

Consider the levels of different features in your grounds, such as the water fountains found in this school's grounds.

Spaces around the outside of the school building are interconnected and allow movement around the grounds when wanted. Different textures add to the range of sensory experiences the children come across around the site.

A sloping path running alongside this pond allows children of different heights to be able to study the pond life with ease.

A path has been created around the boundary of this site allowing pupils to access areas across the site throughout the year.

All pupils should be able to have access to nature on a regular basis.

This interactive sculpture brings delight to pupils who look through it and see spaces they don't expect to see as mirrors reflect light around corners.

Sand play designed for children in wheelchairs is also ideal for younger children to use standing alongside it.

A great way to move between two different levels of the playground.

Wildlife, biodiversity and nature

Evidence is growing as to the importance of everyday contact with nature, especially for children. In *Last Child in the Woods* (2010: 35), Richard Louv states that:

> . . . another emerging body of scientific evidence indicates that direct exposure to nature is essential for physical and emotional health. For example, new studies suggest that exposure to nature may reduce the symptoms of Attention Deficit Hyperactivity Disorder (ADHD), and that it can improve all children's cognitive abilities and resistance to negative stresses and depression.

School grounds are an excellent place for this to happen and the development of these spaces into more biodiverse environments will also ensure that more wildlife visits the sites, thus providing children with more encounters with the natural world.

How to make it work

There are two main strands to success in this area – the development of your grounds to promote biodiversity and the development of access to wildlife for the children.

First, as with all aspects of school grounds developments, make sure you know what you have already have. Even what might appear to be the most barren of grounds will have some areas where wildlife has made a home, and even in the best grounds there are still likely to be changes you can make to encourage more wildlife to live in and visit your site.

Get to know your space; where does the sun rise and set and where does the shade fall within your grounds? Which spots stay wet for long periods/which dry out quickly? Where does the prevailing wind come from and where does litter collect around your site? Make sure you know the main species of trees and shrubs in your grounds as well as any other plants you can identify. Your pupils can also test your soil, for both structure and pH and whether you have a clay, sandy or loam-based soil; whether it is acidic or alkaline will determine what can grow there and what grows naturally.

Local experts will also be able to help you develop a range of habitats and food sources to encourage more wildlife to visit your grounds. This might include wildflower meadows, ponds, streams and wetland areas, hedges and walls, trees and shrubs, heathland and orchards or man-made features such as bird boxes and minibeast hotels. Linking up habitats also helps, so think about how you can join these together, maybe along existing walkways or boundaries.

Remember too to consider how you want to view and study the plants and animals in your grounds. This will not only determine where you position different features but whether you create structures to view the animals – either for them to visit or for you to hide behind. Some ideas might include a bird table within view of a classroom, building a bird hide, creating a dipping platform by your pond, developing wildlife habitats far enough away to not be disturbed by noise and activity but near enough to access easily from the school buildings.

TOP TIPS

- Be inspired by your local area. What grows well locally is likely to do well in your grounds too.
- Make sure whoever maintains your grounds understands your aims. One way to do this is to write a management plan for your whole site then define who is responsible for looking after each area or habitat.
- Think about linking wildlife and biodiversity to other aspects of school life so children have contact with nature every day. This might be through natural play spaces, growing an edible hedgerow, organic approaches to gardening or studying wildlife.

Useful organisations

British Ecological Society – www.britishecologicalsociety.org
The Conservation Volunteers – www.tcv.org.uk
Countryside Council for Wales – www.ccw.gov.uk
Farming and Countryside Education (FACE) – www.face-online.org.uk
Forest Education Initiative – www.foresteducation.org
Landlife – www.wildflower.co.uk
Open Air Laboratories – www.opalexplorenature.org
Outdoor Learning in Scotland –
  http://www.educationscotland.gov.uk/learningteachingandassessment/
  approaches/outdoorlearning/index.asp
RSPB – www.rspb.org.uk
Scottish Natural Heritage – www.snh.org.uk
The Wildlife Trusts – www.wildlifetrusts.org
The Woodland Trust – www.woodlandtrust.org.uk

This pond not only provides an excellent habitat but also provides children with safe access to it for their studies.

As pupils engage more with the natural world around them the more likely they are to want to take care of it, both now and later in life.

A simple, handmade 'minibeast hotel' provides an excellent habitat for many creatures that can be studied in the school's grounds.

Here a spider made by a school celebrates the wildlife found in their grounds and is made from rhododendron branches.

A pond which can be safely accessed by pupils as they study what lives inside it.

Simple traps located around the site allow pupils to study the wildlife that lives in or visits the school's grounds.

A shed cut in half provides this school with a simple bird hide, allowing pupils to study the birds in their local area.

A habitat made specifically to encourage beetles to find a home in the grounds.

Growing

Many schools decide to focus a major part of their school grounds development on growing produce, such as fruit and vegetables. Projects can vary in size from planted up tubs and hanging baskets to the creation of a large allotment area or orchard.

The Royal Horticultural Society (2010: 6) recently commissioned some research to assess the impact of gardening in schools, which showed that gardening in schools encourages children to:

- become stronger, more **active learners** capable of thinking independently and adapting their skills and knowledge to new challenges at school and in the future
- gain a more **resilient, confident and responsible** approach to life so they can achieve their goals and play a positive role in society
- learn **vital job skills** such as presentation skills, communication and team work, and fuel their **entrepreneurial spirit**
- embrace a **healthier, more active** lifestyle as an important tool for success at school and beyond
- develop the ability to **work and communicate with people of all ages** and backgrounds.

How to make it work

As with any development of your grounds you need to think first about what you want to achieve with a growing project, who is going to be involved and particularly importantly who is going to oversee the project and take care of the ongoing maintenance requirements.

Growing projects can focus on after-school activity, developing life-long skills and interests, learning about healthy eating and active living, sustainability and economics or link to different areas of the curriculum – science being the most obvious area for development.

There are many different organisations and individuals who can help you with a growing project. Investigate your local community – you may find a local community garden club or allotment society, parents or grandparents who are keen gardeners and willing to share their enthusiasm and expertise. Local companies such as garden centres may also be happy to share their knowledge, resources or time.

There are also national organisations that can provide information or support for your project (see *Useful organisations* on page 61).

Plan your growing area carefully. If you are developing a significant project the first issue to consider is its location. You will need somewhere sunny and easy to access that won't be destroyed by stray footballs! An outside tap is a necessity and a place to gather a class together and store tools helps. As you become more confident you could expand with a polytunnel or greenhouse, art works, fruit cages and housing for livestock.

TOP TIPS

- Consider the seasons – school holidays can be a problem with crops that need harvesting and watering so plan ahead – for example, anyone coming in and watering over the summer months also gets to take home anything that is ready to pick.
- Don't just think about growing as an out-of-lesson activity. There is much that can be learnt through lessons in your food or flower garden such as the history of plants, the geography of where they come from, the sustainability of using local food over imported food, scientific studies of the requirements of plants to flourish or creative writing and art work.
- Why not cook what you grow? Cooking on a simple campfire, barbecue or even a pizza oven in your grounds will add to the excitement of growing your own fruit and vegetables.

Useful organisations

The Association of Garden Trusts – www.gardenstrusts.org.uk
Garden Organic – www.gardenorganic.org.uk
Growing Schools – www.growingschools.org.uk
The Royal Horticultural Society – www.rhs.org.uk

At this school different members of the local community come together to plant new trees in their grounds.

The arrangement of raised beds, greenhouse and hard standing provide a space that is practical to use in lessons and clubs.

Pupils learn about growing fruit and vegetables; here they are planting seeds for the season ahead.

Compost bins allow schools to recycle plant materials and provide organic compost for their growing areas.

Many schools grow fruit and vegetables whilst in this school garden flowers are also amongst the plants that are grown.

A new building has been created in the grounds of this school that enables staff to take lessons into the grounds and access the nearby planting areas.

The extensive growing area at this school includes raised beds, fruit cages, a polytunnel and chickens.

Polytunnels can help to extend the growing season and provide opportunities to grow crops that might not have been able to be grown outside.

Seating and meeting

School is a key place for children to socialise, to make friends, to observe others and to gain solitude. Seating is key to enabling all these to happen effectively, so it is important that it is well planned, designed, located and maintained and truly takes pupils' needs into account. It is also important to get seating right to enable teaching outside.

Dr Ken Fisher, Educational Planner, Rubida Research, writes about the importance of the structure of teaching and learning environments (2005). While he points out that there are many factors to take into account, there is evidence to show that different seating layouts support different styles of teaching and learning. Whether pupils are being instructed, are collaborating with each other or working independently, different seating layouts will support each approach more effectively.

How to make it work

Consider who is to use the seating, what are they likely to be using it for, when are they using it and where is it needed to be most effective? You may want seating for a specific purpose or to be multifunctional – often the former turns into the latter so it is a good idea to brainstorm all your reasons for wanting seating at the start rather than focusing on one type of seating straight away.

Some of the reasons for wanting seating might include:

- for parents to gather at the beginning and end of the day
- for pupils to socialise, to watch others or be quiet – in small groups or on their own
- for performances or storytelling
- to gather a whole class, or an even larger group for lessons or for assemblies.

Consider the following when you decide where and how to plan your seating:

- Make sure the positioning of seating does not disturb those inside your building – if you want to use seating for lessons do not place it directly outside someone else's classroom.
- Create seating near to features you want to use or study in lessons, so that you can gather your class easily when you are outside.
- Seating for socialising could be close to other activities such as sports courts and pitches, but be careful about flying footballs.
- Think about the prevailing wind, this may influence the location of your seating or you might add shelter to the design, e.g. planting or mesh fencing.
- Consider whether shading from direct sun is needed. Shade can be achieved naturally with planting or more quickly by using tarpaulins and shade sails, which may also provide some shelter from the rain.
- The design of the layout of seating needs to reflect its desired use. For example, bench seating around a tree trunk is aesthetically pleasing but not conducive to socialising. A useful design for seating is based on a horseshoe, but not too large, so that pupils can relate well to each other and the whole group can be addressed at once. This suits outdoor teaching and learning as well as being a useful gathering space for outdoor activities e.g. barbecues, sports day award ceremonies, concerts, displays etc.
- Vary the areas to incorporate large groups or smaller groups of three or four children, and think about the 'feel' of the space – whether more formal or intimate.
- Think about seating that has more than one purpose, e.g. seating attached to planters, seating that also acts as a storage element or rocks used for geology.
- Consider seating that has a 'special' purpose such as 'storytelling seats'. Why not work with an artist or craftsperson to make something unique for your school?
- Use the topography or your site to your benefit – where you have a natural slope think about creating seating that rises up it or create your own amphitheatre.
- Having a store of flexible seating such as picnic blankets, carpet tiles or foam cushions can extend the use of outdoor seating into the winter months.
- Consider using seating that can be moved and changed so that the layout can be altered, thus making it more flexible.
- Always consider the materials you are using; that they are from sustainable sources, they are robust enough to take tough use by pupils and others and that they are easy to maintain.

TOP TIPS

- When planning social seating take a walk around the grounds while the children are out to see where they naturally congregate.
- For maximum flexibility incorporate a mixture of loose, moveable seating as well as fixed permanent seating.
- Consider your seating as a canvas for art work – adding mosaics, recycled rope, painted murals, or just through the materials used in construction.

Useful organisations

Work with local playground equipment suppliers, artists, craftspeople and landscape garden designers. Learning through Landscapes (www.ltl.org.uk) can provide useful contacts.

Moveable seating allows pupils to come together in groups of different sizes and for different types of activity.

Photograph: © Malcolm Cochrane.

A rustic seating area within willow planting and around a fire pit provides an informal seating area for a whole class to gather outside.

Carved stone seats are not only unique to this school but also provide informal seating areas for pupils to meet up.

A unique chair provides a suitable location for a storyteller to sit to address a group of children.

Raised gathering spaces provide particularly special places for children to meet.

A large amphitheatre created within this school's grounds provides a space where large groups can come together for lessons, performances and assemblies.

Straw bales provide a way of creating seating that is changeable yet substantial in form.

A meeting area that is designed to provide shade and shelter as well as seating.

Sustainability and management

Sustainability and management of your grounds go hand in hand; managing your grounds in a sustainable way is good for the environment and will enable your development to endure over a number of years.

Sustainability often refers to making sure the environment is well cared for and able to support all forms of life – and this means humans too! Your school's grounds are an ideal place to establish environmental principles not just for the sake of the environment but to educate your children too. It is not uncommon for schools to teach about the importance of caring for the environment within lessons, but outdoors you can demonstrate how these principles work in practice – a powerful way to communicate your message.

Sustainability also refers to making sure that any new policies or practices are established, reviewed and, if necessary, renewed in such a way that they will endure for the long term.

How to make it work

Developing policies that are clear to understand and implement is key. This might involve drawing up a management plan for the care of your grounds or the way your staff manage playtime; it could involve looking at how schemes of work incorporate activities outside or how your school development plan references the grounds as a whole.

Start by reviewing current policies and plans. Even if you are not wanting to make immediate physical changes to your grounds you should review what you are paying for now – such as your maintenance contract – to make sure that you are getting what you pay for and also that it meets your current needs.

In addition, whenever you create new features or ways of using your grounds, make sure you consider the environmental as well as maintenance implications. Many changes to your grounds will require changes in your maintenance (the day-to-day care of your site) – this could be a new mowing regime to create a meadow; regularly checking new equipment for safety, children getting involved in looking after a growing area or parents regularly getting together to clear out a pond. But making changes to your grounds will also impact on wildlife – you need to ensure that you don't destroy important habitats or sources of food.

Also think about the methods you use for managing your grounds. Are pesticides and artificial fertilisers used, and do you want to continue with these or would you rather use organic methods, for example, making your own compost? You could also look at ways of using water more efficiently – collecting rain in water butts and using drought-tolerant species and mulches to reduce the amount of water required, for example.

Finally, when you are developing your grounds, make sure you consider the origin of the materials you want to use. Timber should be sourced from sustainably managed woods or forests, for example. A good mantra is to 'reduce, reuse, repair and recycle' and to buy local products if you can – including locally grown native plants – and work with local people whenever possible.

Are there other policies that affect how you manage your grounds? How is playtime managed? Have you undertaken appropriate risk assessments or, even better, risk-benefit analyses, of your grounds? Do you have plans for how you will develop the use of your grounds in the future as these will also have an impact on the management of your site.

TOP TIPS

- Audit your current level of sustainability and managements before you make any changes.
- Remember that what you teach in the classroom and what you demonstrate outside in the way you manage your grounds should be consistent.
- Ask advice from local experts if you are not sure what plants, trees, wildlife etc. you already have in your grounds or how best to manage them.

Useful organisations

Eden Project – www.edenproject.com
Global Footprints – www.globalfootprints.org.uk
Sustainable Schools Alliance – www.sustainable-schools-alliance.org.uk/
Sustainable Schools at Sustainability and Environmental Education (SEEd) –
   www.se-ed.co.uk/sustainable-schools/

A school-made irrigation system runs down the hill from a water pump to where it is needed in the garden area.

A change in mowing regime will produce a wildflower meadow over time.

The elements of this dividing line are made from materials taken from the site prior to development.

The use of recycled materials in this wall provides a feature that is unique to this school.

Solar panels can power a range of features in your grounds.

A greenhouse made from empty lemonade bottles collected by pupils in this school.

Pupils have a role in the management of the equipment at the end of playtime.

Collecting water from the roof of a shed to be used to water plants in the grounds.

Community and clubs

School grounds projects are great ways for getting your school community and wider neighbourhood involved in the life of the school. There are many ways different community members can get involved and different people will be able to help you in different ways, so think carefully about what you would like support with and consider who lives and works in your area. Involving the community in running clubs is just one of the ways to use their expertise and enthusiasm.

How to make it work

Below are just some of the ways your local community might get involved in your grounds developments and use:

- Invite members of your community to join your school grounds management group – they may well have useful skills such as bookkeeping or grant application writing.
- Ask your neighbours what they think of your grounds – they may well have gone to the school themselves and will love to be asked about what it was like when they were at school. This is a great way for your pupils to get to know the older members of your community and may well bring inspiration for your future plans.

- Do you have a local expert who can help you with the development plans of your site? Maybe a designer, an artist or craftsperson. You may have someone who represents a local community group who can advise on different types of food plants you could grow or help you make sure that any signage is inclusive for local people.
- When it comes to making changes to your grounds you may need an expert but you may also need many hands to make light work. Ensure that you have someone who is skilled and knowledgeable in charge and run work days where you invite in family and friends to help you with anything from digging a pond to constructing your growing beds.
- Do you have local companies or suppliers who can help? Many companies are keen to support their local community, so find out who is in your area and make friends with them. You never know when this might come in handy.
- You might also plan work days to manage your grounds. This could be a general clean up once a year or a clear-out of the pond or wildlife area, or there could be more specialist tasks if you are lucky enough to have that knowledge available to you.
- The range of clubs you can offer your pupils may well be extended by involving community members. The local allotment society could help with your growing club or parents might come in and help with a den-building club. The local amateur dramatic society could help you develop a drama club whilst a local faith group might be able to look at activities to run with a school faith group outside as well as inside. The clubs you can run will depend on who is available in your local area, but do think creatively about the range of clubs that could use your outside spaces – at different times of year if not all year round.
- There may also be ways the community uses your grounds and this may affect the way you develop your site. This could be planned activity such as sports clubs or uniformed organisations using your grounds for camping, but it might also be unplanned or unwanted visitors and you will need to consider how best to deal with these too.

TOP TIPS

- If you are looking for help in your grounds project ask for specific help. The *Skills audit template* in *Part 4: Resources* shows you just one way of doing this.
- If you have problems getting support start by asking individuals you can rely on. Then ask them to bring one other person along to the next event and gradually build up over time.
- Make sure you thank everyone who helps you and publicise what you have achieved.

Useful organisations

The Conservation Volunteers – www.tcv.org.uk
Groundwork – www.groundwork.org.uk
Information about extended schools – www.direct.gov.uk/en/parents/childcare/ dg_172212
National Confederation of Parent Teachers Associations – www.ncpta.org.uk
Scottish Parent Teacher Council – www.sptc.info
The Wildlife Trusts – www.wildlifetrusts.org.uk

The local community come together to help build this boardwalk structure across the school pond.

Growing provides a way for different generations to come together and learn from each other.

Why not take a range of clubs outside into the grounds – such as music and other arts clubs?

Using the school's grounds for training for members of the local community can be an excellent way of using features within your site.

This school makes the most of using the skills of members of the local community and brings many different people into the grounds to share their skills and knowledge with the pupils.

As the school is located close to an army barracks they often use the skills and resources of the servicemen to help them with the development of their grounds.

Parents come into the school to help clear an area of the grounds.

A member of the local community brings in homing pigeons and pupils map their journey.

Behaviour

Children often become disruptive when they are bored or confined. Through sensitive design and use of the school grounds, however, different behaviours and different learning styles can be accommodated. Research shows, for example, that there is a direct and positive impact on children's behaviour through encouraging play outdoors, and by creating a range of play opportunities (for further guidance, see *Part 3: Heading towards your vision − Play*). Reducing conflicts and tensions in the playgrounds in turn impacts on children's behaviour back in the classroom. Similarly, taking learning outdoors allows children to practise responsible behaviour, and participate in collaborative behaviour, helping them learn how to work together.

A project led by the Forestry Commission Scotland (Groves 2011: 3) found that where natural play elements were introduced into a school's grounds there had been:

- a reduction in the reporting of bullying
- increased opportunities for free, imaginative and creative play
- enhanced social interaction between different groups of children, including between boys and girls, and different age groups.

How to make it work

Despite the clear benefits of play, many schools find playtime a challenge. Badly designed school grounds encourage negative behaviour. Open, unstructured playgrounds become a free-for-all where children compete for space or charge about in frenzied chasing games. Those who do not excel in the skills needed for dominant games are isolated in an environment that doesn't meet their needs. This can lead to low self-esteem. Children's attitudes and behaviour are also strongly affected by the aesthetics of their surroundings.

Making changes need not be costly or time consuming. Many schools, for example, have 'no-go' areas within their grounds. Creating an encouraging environment means moving away from telling children what they can't do and where they can't go and working instead on finding ways in which the children's needs can be addressed. For example, younger children especially favour nooks and crannies for emotional security and comfort, but often these areas (behind the shed, under a bush) are forbidden areas.

Encourage choice in play by taking a fresh look at your grounds and consider variety (intimate, noisy, quiet, large, physical spaces), relaxation (children need to feel safe and supervised but not overlooked), room to move and room for others (including a variety of spaces such as soft and hard, flat and undulating).

Consider zoning your playground (without the use of physical barriers to minimise conflict over use of the space and to make supervision easier). Trial different activities/ different spaces through the use of temporary barriers such as rope or cones.

Lessons outside can have a positive effect on behaviour too. Children who struggle to sit quietly behind a desk are not the only ones to benefit from being outside, where they can engage with the real world in hands-on, creative approaches to learning. Some teachers will have concerns about taking classes outside but time and time again, even the most inexperienced teacher will find that behaviour of some of the most difficult children improves as they find a setting that excites and enthrals them as well as not constraining both their imaginations and movement. The more lessons you take outside and the more you focus on the value of the learning taking place, the more the pupils will accept this as part of their everyday school life. Start small, with quick activities outside as part of a lesson, and build up to extended periods outside and you will see how your pupils respond in the way they behave outdoors.

TOP TIPS

- Involve the whole school community in promoting the value the school places on play. Consider developing a play policy, a simple document that promotes the value your school places on play and on the positive experiences the children who attend can expect to have.
- Create a sense of ownership and responsibility by involving the children in devising a code of conduct for the playground; managing and maintaining areas of the grounds; coming up with new ideas for play; raising funds to be spent on their space etc.

Useful publications and organisations

English government guidance on bullying with reference to playground strategies can be found at https://www.education.gov.uk/publications/eOrdering Download/DFE-RR098.pdf
Anti-Bullying Alliance – www.anti-bullyingalliance.org.uk
Beat Bullying – www.beatbullying.org

Ensuring lessons are engaging will help ensure that pupils can be trusted to work sensibly without constant, close supervision.

Providing nooks and crannies can enable children to find places to go and calm down when they need to be alone.

On a silent walk pupils live up to expectations as they sit quietly in the wood, demonstrating that they can be trusted to behave as required outside.

The outdoor environment offers an ideal setting for creative and innovative lessons such as an actor performing the tale of the Pied Piper of Hamlin, providing an engaging lesson for pupils.

Even in the dark pupils can be trusted to behave when activities are engaging and stimulating.

At the conclusion of their playtimes children take on responsibility for clearing up the equipment they have used.

Natural and open-ended play features often encourage more cooperative play between boys and girls.

Engaging pupils in the process of reviewing and developing their grounds will help them to find a sense of ownership and care for the site.

Part 4: Resources

This section of *Learn and Play Out* is full of resources to help you develop your grounds in a way that is unique to you but also by learning from what others have done before. There is a copy of the audit tool to get you started, case studies and images to inspire you as you develop your own solutions and activities to help you undertake the survey of your grounds and involve everyone in the process of change.

All the printed resources in this section can also be found on the accompanying CD-ROM so that you can repeat the audit over the year and print and share all the activity ideas, case studies and images as you need them.

How to use the resources

The audit tool is designed to help you find out where your strengths and weaknesses lie.

The case studies and images correspond in theme to the 11 themes highlighted in the audit. This means that when you discover an area you want to focus on within your developments you can find inspiration by seeing what another school has achieved. Every school is different and you should not feel you need to repeat exactly the work of another school. Instead, the idea is for you to be inspired by what is possible and think about how you can apply some of the principles to your own school site and develop ideas that fit your particular needs.

You can also use the case studies and images to help get your school community supporting the development. For example, you may decide to use some of the images when creating mood boards, or use the case studies to encourage parents and governors to get on board.

The activities are designed to help you all the way through the process of developing your grounds. Some will help you to undertake the audit; others will help you work out how to plan the next steps of what you are going to do. Throughout *Part 2: The process of change*, these activities are highlighted so you can see when to use them. You may also choose to use the basic ideas behind the activities but develop them and use them in different ways. They are designed to get your whole school community involved in the development of your grounds and many can also be used to support the delivery of the curriculum and after-school clubs.

All of *Part 4* is there to help you with your project – to help you through the process of change by making you look more closely at what you already have, by helping you identify possible solutions to issues and by inspiring you to make the best possible changes to your grounds.

About the audit tool

Most schools will have some idea about where their strengths and weaknesses lie, where they have problems and whether they would like to develop and use their grounds further. However, this can also cloud your view as to what else is good, bad or ugly about your site. Therefore, in order for you to get a good overview of your grounds, we have provided you with an audit tool that will help you develop a more objective view of your grounds and maybe uncover some examples of good practice or areas that you need to address that you didn't know about.

The audit tool can be found on the accompanying CD-ROM within the folder *Audit* under the Excel file labelled: Audit Tool. When you open the tool the first spreadsheet will give you clear instructions on how to complete the audit and also guidance on how to print pages should you wish to.

The audit starts by requesting some basic information about your school. This should be straightforward to collect and may help when you are putting together applications for funding or looking at other schools with similar issues.

Once this information has been completed there are three general sections about your grounds for you to complete. One looks at the current use of your site, one at the design issues and one at the management of your grounds. Gathering information here will give you an overview of the state of your grounds and help you start to see where your strengths and weaknesses lie.

School information

	A	B	C	D	E	F	G
1	Name of school						
2							
3	Address of school						
4							
5							
6	Our community is	in a city	in a town	in a village	coastal	other	
7	When our school was built:	main buildings:		permanent changes:		temporary changes:	
8	Our site is	very restricted	small in size	medium in size	large in size		
9		very sunny	quite sunny	quite shaded	very shaded		
10		very windy	quite windy	not at all windy			
11	Our grounds have	only hard surfacing	mainly hard surfacing	a good mix of hard and soft surfacing	mainly soft surfacing	all soft surfacing	
12		a large playground	a small playground	more than one playground	a small field	a large field	
13		clay soil	sandy soil	loamy soil	acid soil	alkaline soil	
14		only flat areas	some slopes or hills	lots of hills or slopes	a steep incline		

Overview of use

	A	B	C	D	E	F
3		Use				
4		General overview of the use of your outside space - a more detailed review can be found later in this audit				
5	Do teachers take lessons outside? - Please circle which applies to you	once a year or less	once a year to once a term	about twice a term	about once a month	every week
6	Where do they take place - please name spaces and places you use					
7	When do they happen?	Autumn term	Spring term	Summer term		
8	Are there particular features used for teaching? - please name these					
9	How are the grounds used for play and socialising? - a more detailed review can be found later in this audit					
10	Are there different groups that use the grounds for playing and socialising?	pupils	siblings	parents	staff	the local community
11	Are there particular areas that are used at different times of day, year, or for specific activities? - please describe these					

School layout and design

	A	B	C	D	E	F	G	H
4	What is the signage like at the entrance to the school?							
5	Is it clear?							
6	Is it welcoming?							
7	The next few questions look at how pupils move around your site							
8	Note on a plan existing pathways and how they are used							
9	Show on an overlay where the current desire lines are (these are routes that are commonly used but might not be formal paths e.g. the most regularly used route from the main exit to the pond)							
10	Note how the formal paths are used too							
11	Note on your plan entrances and exits from the building and who uses them and why							
12	Note the different entrances to your site - who uses these and when?							
13	The next few questions look at the style of your grounds							
14	How might you describe the style of your grounds? There are some options here to help you think about this	urban	rural	formal	informal	historical	busy	open
15	Have you had a designer or artist involved in the design of your grounds or specific features within it? Please describe this							
16	Do you have a variety of meeting spaces around your grounds? There is a section in the audit for more details on this	for the whole school	for classes	for small groups	for ones and twos			
17	Do you have specific features designed for play and recreation? - please name them							
18	Do your grounds support specific types of play?	natural play	creative play	physical play	co-operative play	solitary play		
19	Do you have features and spaces designed specifically for sport? Please name them							
	Do you have specific features designed							

Management of the site

◇ 3	A	B	C	D	E	F	G	H
				Management				
4	The physical management of your grounds (grass cutting, shrub pruning, problems fixed etc.) There is a section in the audit for more details on this	is excellent	is good	is OK	is poor	is very poor		
5	How is the outdoors planned into teaching and learning?							
6	Is outdoor learning in your development plan?							
7	Is outdoor learning incorporated into schemes of work?	in all our schemes of work	in the majority of our schemes of work	in some of our schemes of work	in none of our schemes of work			
8	Does one of your staff have responsibility for outdoor learning?							
9	How is playtime managed?							
10	How many staff manage break and lunch times?							
11	Where are they positioned?							
12	Have they had effective training?							
13	How do they interact with pupils?							
14	How is the playground organised for different activities?							
	Is all the space							

To really want to make a difference to your grounds, however, you will need to dig deeper to find out more of the detail of what is working in your grounds and what you need to focus on more in the future. Moving on, you will find 11 tables, each with a different theme. You will notice that these are the same themes highlighted in *Parts 3* and *4* of the toolkit and, when complete, they will help you see what you should be looking at within these areas and point you towards the resources that will support your project.

Completing the audit

For each section you will see a list of statements or questions down the left-hand side. Across the table you will then find answers either in individual boxes or as headings for a column, depending on the issues being addressed. Each heading will have an associated value or score with it. Find the heading that most closely reflects your school grounds and assign the related score. Sometimes the scores are weighted and you will be asked to multiply by a given figure – do this to get your score for that individual question. The scores will be automatically added up at the end of the rows.

Once you have your final totals for each section turn to the final section in the audit which is the summary section. In this section, your scores will have filtered through for each of the areas you have focused on. You can then see from the summary form whether you are doing well in this area or whether you need to work more on this theme.

Completing the tables

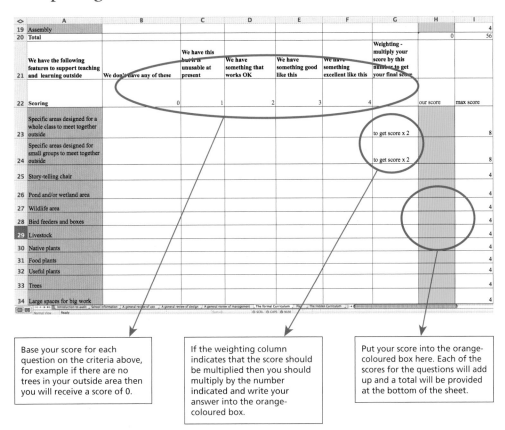

Base your score for each question on the criteria above, for example if there are no trees in your outside area then you will receive a score of 0.

If the weighting column indicates that the score should be multiplied then you should multiply by the number indicated and write your answer into the orange-coloured box.

Put your score into the orange-coloured box here. Each of the scores for the questions will add up and a total will be provided at the bottom of the sheet.

Summary page

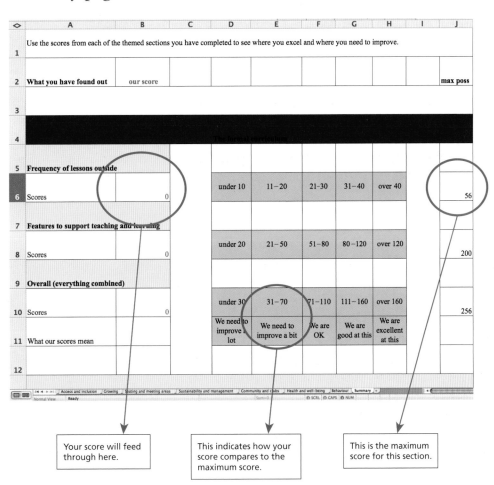

Your score will feed through here.

This indicates how your score compares to the maximum score.

This is the maximum score for this section.

What happens next?

You may find more than one area needs addressing and it might be that in focusing on one area you will benefit another – so try to look at as many aspects as you can in the audit of your grounds, even if you then focus in on only a few aspects. Remember that you still need to have an overview of your grounds' development, even if you then focus on one area for development at a time, as all areas will impact on each other.

In *Part 3* of the toolkit you will find out why each aspect of school grounds is important and how you can go about developing them further. There are also top tips and places and people to go to for further information and support on each theme. In addition, in *Part 4*, you will find case studies and images to provide inspiration under each theme. Use these to help you develop your grounds then review where you get to by repeating the audit to see if your scores have improved and what you need to focus on next.

Case study 1: Coombes CE Primary School

The school

Coombes CE Primary School is a large primary school in Arborfield, Berkshire. The proportion of pupils with special educational needs and/or disabilities is below the national average and a small proportion of pupils are eligible for free school meals. The school has part-time nursery provision.

Key focus

The development of this site shows how school grounds can be used to support **teaching and learning**, through an experiential curriculum.

Who was involved?

The school grounds at the Coombes school have been developed over a period of 40 years led primarily by the school's recently retired headteacher. In that time, however, all teaching staff have embraced the potential of the space for teaching. The school also benefits from many carefully managed relationships with the local community and parents.

Project overview

The use and development of the school's grounds as a teaching environment has been a constant feature since it opened and many elements of it are integral to their holistic approach to learning.

For example, a small flock of sheep is kept by the school, providing many learning opportunities. Pupils quickly become familiar with the sheep as they are moved around the site to graze and witness the birth of lambs and the shearing of the flock. Older pupils then work with parents and volunteers to wash, dry, work and dye the fleeces, which are then spun into wool on Textiles Day.

To further develop opportunities for learners to experience the natural world the school has developed a labyrinth, three ponds and a wetland area, greatly increasing the range and diversity of flora and fauna available to study. The size and design of these ponds allow for different sorts of learning experiences, with one having a low wall and flat surfaces for working whilst another larger one has a boardwalk running round the edges of the deepest part.

A significant feature of the grounds is the geology trail which has been gradually developed to include large rocks and standing stones of different types from across the country. Some of these rocks have been placed to form 'Coombeshenge', but all are used by pupils as spaces for learning, playing and socialising.

Key messages

Recognise that using and developing the grounds to deliver experiential learning requires the support and cooperation of parents and neighbours. From its earliest days the Coombes school has embraced its local community. This philosophy of development and evolution has continued as all staff recognise the outside space as a living classroom rather than a project with a clearly defined end. Four decades of inspiration and dedication have created a teaching and learning environment that has become the subject of international study.

Case study 2: Caledonia Primary

The school

Caledonia Primary in Baillieston, Glasgow, has a roll of 177 children, with another 24 attending the separate language unit on site.

Key focus

The development of this site shows how changes to the landscape and the provision of loose play materials can enhance children's experience of unstructured, open-ended **play**.

Who was involved?

Strong support from the headteacher and the senior management team was key to the success of the project. Children, teaching staff and parents were engaged in a series of consultations and activities around current use of their outside space, its current limitations and the school's future aspirations. Playground supervisors and the janitor were engaged and involved from the outset. A Learning through Landscapes project advisor supported the school throughout this process and the services of a landscape designer were sought in relation to the creation of the design plan and the management of the contract. Parents were involved in supporting the school in a practical way through their involvement in creating some of the features and planting trees.

Project overview

During the initial consultation and observation phase many children reported that football dominated the playground. Popular suggestions for improvements included a tunnel, a den, swinging, climbing, sliding, quiet areas and creating areas where football was not allowed. Staff commented, 'We would like pupils to have the opportunity to explore nature by climbing, jumping and balancing – as well as opportunities to play around, behind, over and through and to engage in fantasy play.'

The school decided to combine these wishes into a whole-school plan and work towards it in stages. Initial developments included the provision of:

Photographs: © Malcolm Cochrane.

Photographs: © Malcolm Cochrane.

- 'hobitats' (mounds and tunnels) – three large grass-covered tunnels (two of which are enclosed) provide a vantage point for running from, jumping off and observing the playground.
- a large-scale sand area and barrels – in front of the 'hobitats' is a large sand area where children of all ages engage in open-ended play. Barrels in the middle collect water.
- interesting grass areas – soil remaining from digging out the sand pit was used to build mounds and terraces in the grass to create a natural amphitheatre. Varied mowing regimes encourage biodiversity and create places for the children to hide in the longer grass.
- loose materials – tree stumps can be moved and used in games or as seats.
- changes to play supervision – children now have the choice to go out in wet weather and play in all areas, which has resulted in the number of disciplinary issues falling as the children look out for each other.

Key messages

'Sustained, engaged play that the children have control of' can be achieved by engaging the children in the process of change. Staff and children were involved in developing a risk-benefit assessment for the space and the children were active in developing a code of conduct based on supporting each other through play.

Case study 3: Neumark Grundschule Primary

The school

Neumark Grundschule Primary in Berlin is an urban school serving a mainly immigrant population. Where once there was an all-asphalt site now there is a mix of natural play features and art elements transforming the atmosphere within the grounds.

Key focus

The development of this site shows how a school grounds development can support the **hidden curriculum,** transformed from a dull, urban environment into a magical space for children to play and spend time.

Who was involved?

The pupils at this school were key to the success of the project. The school engaged with designers and educationalists to find out what they wanted to be able to do in their school grounds. Pupils visited other school grounds and created models and designs for their own grounds which the designers then interpreted into the final plans.

Pupils have since been involved in creating a multitude of art works that also help to create a welcoming and pupil-focused space. Some of these art works have pupil names alongside them, acknowledging their part in the development of the site.

Project overview

The school building is a multistorey block dating back to 1889 and before the changes the grounds surrounding the building were asphalt with a line of three trees.

The changes included altering the topography of the site and creating small areas with different activities available in each area. Areas are delineated by curving walls made from a mixture of materials including stone, brick and pottery with trees and shrubs planted throughout. Sculptures – made of stone and wood and created by pupils and artists – are dotted around the site. These are used both as art features in themselves but also places to sit informally.

Pathways, both constructed and worn by use, lead between the spaces, and uneven wooden and rock steps lead up and down. There are places for seating around the site, some built into the walls, others created so that several children can sit talking to each other at a time, rather than sitting in straight rows.

Sand rather than grass is a well-used surface and the use of trees and shrubs with seating underneath in the shade help create a calm, yet stimulating environment where children feel safe and are allowed to use their imaginations as they play.

Key messages

While this project received funding enabling it to be completed in one hit, the majority of the work is replicable in most school grounds, including:

- a series of small spaces across the site for children to spend time in
- the use of trees and shrubs to create a natural feel to the space as well as forming shade under which children can play and socialise
- a wide use of natural materials – particularly wood, stone, water and sand – to help create an inviting, natural atmosphere within the city
- engaging children in the design and development process to develop a sense of ownership and belonging for pupils from a neighbourhood with a very high immigrant population.

Case study 4: Echline Primary

The school

Echline Primary in South Queensferry, Scotland, has a roll of approximately 300 pupils. It was built roughly 30 years ago and six years ago a new nursery building was built in the grounds. Initially it had large areas of tarmac, substantial grassed areas and some mature trees.

Key focus

The development of this site shows how school grounds can support children's **health and wellbeing**. Prior to this, the grounds were mainly used for ball games, sports day and the occasional gym lesson.

Who was involved?

Management responsibility for the project was given to the deputy headteacher. Her responsibilities included consulting with each class and pupil council member on what they wanted to do outside, developing design ideas, keeping everyone informed, employing contractors, organising volunteers and finally signing off the work. She then prioritised the ideas and sought funding and free resources or labour. The school community was kept up to date through newsletters and an information board and the

ideas discussed with the parent/staff association. A skills audit and fundraising plan were put in place.

Project overview

As funding was successful, design ideas were implemented over a ten-year period. These have included the installation of a natural wood trim trail, a winding woodland walk which doubles as a bike track, two traversing walls of varying difficulty and a zoned area for 'wheeled' activities. To help support children's emotional wellbeing, access to nature has been high on the agenda. A pond has been established, a bird box and camera installed, local and exotic plants added to the grounds and a wild woodland area with log seating can now be accessed. Turfed areas are left unmown so the children can experience close contact with long grass, and boundary hedging, new trees and an orchard area have also been added to the site. Various sized planters growing herbs and vegetables allow children to learn about healthy eating.

Key messages

Teaching outdoors is just as important as playtimes for getting children physically active and encouraging contact with nature. Initially staff were reluctant to take their lessons outside and required a good deal of support. By using many of the Learning through Landscapes activity sheets and planning outdoor weeks, backed by display boards to celebrate success, staff gradually gained confidence. They now automatically look for opportunities to take learning outdoors and now plan outdoor learning in all areas of the curriculum. Playground supervisors had anxieties regarding more adventurous play but as the opportunities for play increased they reported less bullying and fights.

Case study 5: Delamere Primary School

The school

Delamere Primary School in Cheshire is for children aged 2–11 with statements of special educational needs due to severe or profound and multiple learning difficulties, physical and sensory impairments or autism.

Key focus

The development of this site shows a school grounds development can achieve **access and inclusion** so all children can experience the outdoors.

Who was involved?

The vision of the senior management team was vital in overcoming perceived barriers to taking their children outside. Pupils at the school have contact with a wide range of adults and the school spent

time creating a whole-school ethos. Through creating links with businesses such as the Trafford Centre, Sainsbury's and Kellogg's, fundraising and collecting donations of time and resources the school worked closely with a range of contractors.

Project overview

Every class has access to space outside their classroom and joint use of a large field. The developments included a mixture of large- and small-scale improvements with a focus on open-ended play allowing each class to personalise the spaces. The six principles of inclusive design are evident throughout the grounds:

- **Diversity and difference** – there are a variety of spaces from small secluded corners to large open spaces and the design capitalises on these. Paths open up the field, nooks and crannies have been painted to create inviting small spaces and all equipment is open-ended and flexible – such as the viewing platform that can be turned into a castle or a pirate ship.
- **Ease of use** – a large clear roof over a courtyard allows free-flow play while enabling children to feel temperature changes; fixings on posts and walls enable temporary shelters to be constructed and the play barn was modified – removing the floor so there would be no lip that wheelchair users would struggle with, posting holes were cut in a wall, transient art frames built on the window ledges and parts of the roof replaced with coloured panels to promote different uses of the space.
- **Freedom of choice** – much of the design allows pupils to use the site as independently as possible – for example, raised beds for wheelchair users, tactile markers along paths and simpler adaptations such as beaters attached to the musical instruments to allow them to be found easily!
- **Quality** – unique adaptations can be seen throughout. For example, a bespoke sand/water feature – created by climbing rock moulded to support children sitting/lying in the sand pit and allowing safe access to water.
- **Legibility and predictability** – the layout is clear and simple with consistent landmarks (wooden poles) or textured strips underfoot for orientation.
- **Safety** – the environment feels safe with clear sightlines and secure fencing but offers exciting and challenging play. A large swing and a raised deck in the Early Years' area offer height and speed while a wildflower meadow and areas of long grass allow immersion into the natural world.

Key messages

Making personal support available can help all teachers increase the way they use their outdoor space. Here, the outdoors is now a focus for the whole school – in forward planning, termly meetings and in-service training – with an expectation that it is used regularly. As one member of staff commented: 'Teachers and staff are our best resource, once they see the benefits of going outside the barriers seem less daunting.'

Case study 6: Oliver's Battery Primary School

The school

Oliver's Battery Primary School in Winchester, Hampshire, has extensive school grounds offering a variety of habitats and opportunities. These include two large playing fields, a small wood, chalk grassland and native trees.

Key focus

The development of this site shows how a school grounds project can support **wildlife, biodiversity and nature** through conservation of the natural landscape.

Who was involved?

The school investigated the skills that parents had and worked with their grounds staff to make changes to the way in which the school grounds were being managed. These efforts were coordinated by one teacher, along with the support of the senior management. The children contributed to the decision-making process through the newly formed eco school council.

Project overview

There were several areas that had huge potential to enable children to understand conservation of the landscape around them.

The first project was to install a mixed mowing regime to enable meadow areas to complement sports pitches and footpaths. These longer grass areas are cut after August each year and the grass collected to mimic the more ideal management of grazing livestock. By cutting this late the flowers, seeds and herbs can benefit the pollinating insects and increase the diversity of plants growing in the area over time. With longer grass areas there was a need to manage any encroaching scrub and this is an ongoing conservation task for older pupils. These areas enable children to come into close contact with orchids and other rarely seen plants and insects.

The school is set on the hill overlooking the city of Winchester. However, lack of management meant the views of the city and surrounding area had been lost. The school worked with parents to manage an overgrown beech hedge in order to create views and enable the staff to interpret the landscape in which the children lived.

The woodland in the school grounds had also been unused for some time. With help from grounds staff and parents two woodland ponds were opened up. One is being managed as a woodland pond while the other has been cleared to enable light to get to the water and encourage a different range of wildlife. The ponds have been made safe and are now used to study pond life. Woodland paths and clearings have been created to enable the children play and learn in these areas.

The school grounds leader was concerned that teaching staff wouldn't have the time or expertise to develop the resources for using in the school grounds. She therefore made a number of resources available on their website and a variety of trails have been established, including a 'berry trail' for identifying different berries in the grounds; a 'spring trail' for identifying early signs of spring, and a 'legs trail' for identifying animals and insects and counting up legs.

In addition the school now offers a theme-based curriculum, with more opportunities to use the outdoors.

Key messages

Being more connected to the outdoors changes the way the children look at the world around them: 'The children have really slowed down, they take their time and are much more aware and observant.' The school was aware and open about their limitations and actively sought realistic ways to overcome the barriers of time, skills and expertise, resulting in giving children more opportunities to understand the conservation of the landscape around them.

Case study 7: Comberbach Primary School

The school

Comberbach Primary School is situated in the rural village of Comberbach, Cheshire. The school is completely inclusive and many of the pupils travel from further afield to attend.

Key focus

The development of this site shows how school grounds can support **growing.** The school received a Big Lottery Award for the project and has successfully reached Level IV in the RHS Campaign for School Gardening. It has also won third prize in Cheshire West and Chester Council Schools in Bloom competition.

Who was involved?

The school has a trained horticulturalist and professional gardener leading the project with a volunteer helper and lots of enthusiastic pupils! They also invite parents and other grown-ups to join in their gardening efforts as well as getting advice from local experts.

The school has invested in raised beds made from recycled plastic, a tumbler composter and rainwater butts. With the Big Lottery Award, new boundary fencing, a greenhouse and a shed have been installed as well as providing essential gardening equipment for the project. The school has also received support from local businesses who have donated plants and equipment for the kitchen garden. They have invited local residents to join in with their gardening efforts – they are very keen that the garden will be a place to bring young and old together.

Project overview

Each class has a raised bed to grow a variety of vegetables, flowers and fruits with gardening sessions run throughout the whole school, with an emphasis on sustainability in the gardening activities being practised. The garden is now being used by teachers in their curriculum teaching across KS1 and KS2 subject areas. The garden is also proving very productive with one year's harvest of new potatoes totalling 20 kg! These potatoes flew off the Kitchen Garden stall at the Comberbach Village Fete. All crops produced in the garden have been sampled both at school and at home.

Class projects involving the garden have included Year 4 pupils designing and cultivating a raised bed with the theme of 'The Vegetable Olympics' for a local schools competition.

The school has continued to involve its local community in its gardening with Year 5 pupils running an open day garden event which local residents and VIPs attended. Parents, grandparents and local residents have taken part in an RHS 'Get Your Grown-ups Growing' event, with the Reception class. In addition, an expert horticulturalist from the local college visited the school and taught the children about plant pests and diseases.

Key messages

Growing can link with all aspects of the curriculum. Here, pupils are learning about growing their own food, the benefits of eating locally produced fresh fruit and vegetables, and about sustainable gardening techniques – including recycling, water conservation and soil management and the impact on the environment. And across the school, teachers have embraced the academic links. Working alongside older generations, gardening has encouraged the sharing of knowledge and experience between young and old in the local community and has helped to foster a sense of wellbeing and community pride in the school.

Case study 8: Catton Primary School

The school

Catton Primary School was formed when Catton Grove First School and Catton Grove Middle School were brought together in 2007. The school is situated in Norfolk and has over 500 children on its roll.

Key focus

The development of this site shows how school grounds can include **seating and meeting** spaces for a range of different sized groups and for different purposes.

Who was involved?

In August 2001, Catton Grove Middle School was burned to the ground so a new school had to be built. The architects worked with the school to develop the new school building and grounds together – so that the inside and outside spaces worked as one, rather than as two separate elements.

Project overview

When the school was rebuilt, the way that seating and meeting places were incorporated into the design of the outside spaces was considered very carefully, with the outside spaces linked to internal spaces. An example of this is how quiet seating spaces were created outside the library, where children are allowed to take their books to read outside. The seats and a gazebo in this space were created by professional wood sculptors based in Suffolk and are unique to the school. Seats are made from logs with heads and limbs of creatures subtly carved into them; planting, art and structures around the seating enclose the spaces making them more intimate and pleasant to spend time in.

While the seating outside the library is designed to take small groups of pupils, there is seating elsewhere around the site that has been created for a range of purposes and sizes of group. Where there are small corners between walls of the building, seating has been provided where just two pupils can sit and chat. Further into the grounds picnic benches have been provided for pupils to eat their lunch or work at. However, even the design of these seats is unusual – designed around a circular table with four bench seats rather than two long benches running alongside a table in the middle. These make talking with friends and collaborative working much easier.

As well as spaces for small groups to meet there is a larger area of seating that can take a couple of classes at a time. Gently tiered wooden benches form a series of semi-circles all facing towards a front space which can be used for performances, lessons or assemblies.

More benches can be found as you tour the grounds, carefully positioned under pergolas or alongside planted areas to ensure comfort and seclusion.

Key messages

Thinking about how seating is to be used can result in the development of different styles of seating across your site. While this school was able to consider its inside and outside spaces together as part of a rebuilding process, many of its ideas and solutions to seating and meeting needs can be taken on board by any school. For example, the positioning of seating outside the library has encouraged pupils to take their reading outside – something they have found many boys have enjoyed. Different types of seating across the site meet a specific need and therefore have different features in their design. Some of this seating was 'off the shelf' whilst other elements were designed specifically for the site. The result is a site that can be used successfully by whole classes, small groups and individuals for learning, for play and for socialising.

Case study 9: Lower Fields Primary School

The school

Lower Fields Primary School in Bradford, West Yorkshire, is a mixed, comprehensive community primary school serving a diverse community. The school has a bright, modern building set in extensive grounds. The site contains more species of trees than any other school in Bradford.

Key focus

The development of this site shows how school grounds can support **sustainability.**

Who was involved?

A sustainability development worker has been leading the project. There are also links and partnerships with local residents and businesses and the grounds have become a resource for the school and wider community for both learning and leisure.

The grounds are a focus for work not only for the pupils and staff of the school but also local residents and local business. There is an 18-strong gardening club and

each class also has its own growing bed. Produce is used in tasting sessions and by kitchen staff in school meals.

Project overview

The school has extensive grounds and with different areas, each with its own function and atmosphere. There is a large growing area with fruit trees and bushes and growing beds. The orchard was planted in 2005 and there are raised beds and a polytunnel. Further around the site through trees and bushes is the school's wildlife area. Rolled stone and mown paths lead to a pond, seating areas and a storytelling chair.

The school reinforces its sustainable principles by sourcing and preparing all their food locally – including some from the school's own gardens. The kitchen has a wormery and composts its own waste, along with garden waste. The school also has a 1,000-litre water butt connected to the roof for watering the gardens.

A pack of resources and information linking the grounds to the curriculum is available for staff to use ensuring that the grounds are not only environmentally sustainable but that strategies and resources have been put in place to ensure they are used for years to come.

Key messages

'If you want things to really happen or for changes to count you have to invest in staff.' By doing this, the school has been able to fulfil one of its main aims: 'to equip their pupils with the knowledge, interest and skills they need to address the wider issues of climate change and sustainability as they go through their education and eventually into the workforce'.

Case study 10: Tenby Junior School

The school

Tenby Junior School in Pembrokeshire, Wales, is situated on the outskirts of the town. Its catchment extends to outlying villages. The site has a large woodland area within it, which has been developed to support both learning and wellbeing.

Key focus

The development of this site shows how a school grounds project can have a strong element of community **engagement.**

Who was involved?

The overall aim has been to develop the grounds for both learning and recreation and for the whole school to make the most of a valued asset. The school has carried out a number of developments over the years, each with a different focus and working with a variety of groups, individuals and organisations. The Prince's Trust created a walkway through the wood and is due to return to the school to upgrade the path. The new pond was created with help from the Fire Brigade, the local rugby club and an international construction company, and parents developed the 'night-line'. Through this work every child in the school benefits from direct access to nature and the school strengthens its links to the local community.

The nature area has featured in the school's development plan for the last five years. The current priority is to ensure complete accessibility for disabled pupils into the woodland and the Roundhouse classroom. The local Round Table have made an ongoing commitment to sponsor this initiative and carry out the physical work. The Rotary are erecting the fence around the new orchard with a financial contribution from the Round Table, and the Prince's Trust in Pembroke put the boardwalk into the nature area. These are powerful examples of the community working together for the good of their children's local school.

Project overview

The school has focused on their grounds for a number of years to make the most of their natural resources, especially the large woodland and stream that bounds the north of the site. There is enormous support and enthusiasm for the use of the outdoors across the staff and among parents and the wider community.

The woodland is the most popular area for learning. Within this relatively extensive area the school has built a turf-roofed roundhouse that can accommodate a whole class. Also in the woods is the 'hidden' classroom, an informal space with log seating where large groups of children can gather. In the summer months this is hidden by the thick foliage of the surrounding trees and shrubs to create a secret dell.

A 'night-line' has been created in the woodland. This is a rope trail running through the woods that pupils can follow blindfolded, as part of PSE. The woods also include two ponds, the upper one with a large dipping platform.

What was learnt?

Getting pupils actively involved in planning and decision-making and in developing and making full use of the site, combined with support from the local community, ensures that grounds continue to be developed and used throughout the life of the school. Tenby Junior School is a school that celebrates its place in the local community through its grounds. Extensive records of their work in press cuttings, images and displays commemorate and record what has been achieved.

Case study 11: Thornlie Primary School

The school

Thornlie Primary School is located in a deprived area of North Lanarkshire and has a current roll of 125 children. The grounds are extensive with two areas of tarmac and a large area of green space.

Key focus

The development of this site shows how school grounds can help to improve **behaviour** by creating opportunities for children to build and explore, climb and jump, to be immersed and in contact with natural materials, make decisions, take risks, work together and test themselves.

Who was involved?

Strong support from the headteacher and the senior management team was key to the success of the project. Children, teaching staff and parents were engaged in a series of consultations and activities to explore how they currently used the outside space and how they would like to use it. Playground supervisors and the janitor were involved and a Learning through Landscapes project advisor supported the school throughout this process. A landscape designer helped with the creation of the design plan and management of the contract. External support was sourced where required, for example bush craft workshops, a willow worker and various artists.

Project overview

Risk, adventure, shelter building, natural play materials, fire and support for the Curriculum for Excellence – all are components of the school's new playground which stimulates learning, develops confidence, improves health and enables urban children to develop a love for the natural. The headteacher says: 'This project builds on work we have already done, and takes us a step closer to seeing a playground that encourages bravery, challenge, creativity, and imagination. It's not just about the transformation of a physical landscape but a cultural one.'

Developing such an ambitious approach to play involved more than providing new features. The school developed policies and risk-benefit frameworks, invested in training and liaised with parents and the school estate managers.

New resources include a climbing tree, a fire pit, willow tunnels, loose materials, a large sand area and varied planting and mowing regimes.

A comparison of pre- and post-project observations demonstrate improvements in physical activity, social interaction and creativity, and the value of what's been done is measurable in terms of attainment, attendance and – most significantly for the school – behaviour. The headteacher says:

> Children who come to us haven't always been well guided in how to sort out conflict. Previously we have never had a year with no suspensions and a number of these have 'started' in the playground. We have had zero exclusions this session, and we have a vision of the 'new' playground not as a source of anxiety but as a source of resolution – as well as fun.

Play is important for its own sake at Thornlie but staff have noticed the impact it has in the classroom too. Teachers come out during break and notice that 'children learn when given freedom and opportunities to think for themselves'.

Key messages

Involving children is key to promoting ownership and enjoyment and helping to support positive behaviour. At Thornlie, for example, the children took part in marking out the areas where resources would go, sourcing materials, planting willow, painting and taking part in construction workshops and workshops involving tools. The school is aware others may feel that what they have achieved is unattainable, but their message is clear – 'make a start – we make the path by walking'.

Activity 1: Observation

One of the best ways to see how your grounds are used is simply by observation. Below are just some techniques you can use to observe what is happening in your grounds:

- **Make a plan** of your grounds and observe how individuals move around the grounds during playtimes. You can focus on one individual at a time and for a limited period or the whole of a breaktime. Mark on the map where they go and note if they stay put in any particular place for a period of time. Note what they do and where they do it. Do this for several people from across the school community, ideally over a number of days and even at different times of year, and/or in different weather conditions.
- **Use photographs** of moments in time – take them from the same places in the grounds at different times of day to see how the grounds are used throughout the day.
- **Video** is a useful way to record what is going on in the grounds. If you make simple observations at specific times it is often surprising what you miss! If you make videos, however, when played back you can often spot something in the background that you wouldn't have otherwise noticed!
- **Finding out how specific features are currently used** is also very useful. Is the play equipment really getting use that is proportionate to its cost or would future development be better focused on different types of provision?

Activity 2: Creating a breaktime diary

Use this activity to gather information about how different year groups and boys and girls each use their school grounds during breaktime. The activity could also be repeated throughout the year to see how different seasons affect play.

What you need

- a large sheet of plain paper or card
- crayons, paints etc. Pictures from magazines or drawn by the pupils representing different activities
- stickers or similar for recording.

Preparation

- Encourage discussion about the different kinds of games/activities pupils take part in at breaktime. With older pupils discuss too the different spaces within the school grounds and what activities generally take place where.
- Find pictures from magazines or encourage pupils to create their own pictures of these different activities.
- Either individually or in small groups, get pupils to prepare a large sheet of paper or card representing each day of the week across one axis and each activity along the other. Decorate it with appropriate pictures. The chart could also include tick boxes for different outdoor spaces, and an opportunity to record the weather each day.

What to do

The aim is for each pupil to record the different games/activities they have taken part in during each breaktime over the period of one week. Provide different coloured stickers or crayons for girls and boys.

Extensions

- Using maths and/or ICT skills, find different ways of analysing and representing the information gathered – for example, most and least popular activities, the differences and/or similarities between boys' and girls' activities, the impact of the weather on activities etc.
- Make temporary changes to the school grounds – for example, restricting access to certain areas, changing flow with temporary barriers – and create a new breaktime diary to evaluate the effect.

Activity 3: Tour of your grounds

Walking around the school site is often the best way to prompt people's thoughts and help them to think about their site. There are a number of different ways this can be done, and the best method will depend on who is undertaking this task and the information you want to gather.

- Groups of pupils can take a tour of the grounds and record their thoughts:
  - o these can be prompted by written questions
  - o pupils can imagine they are taking a celebrity on a tour and show them the areas that might be of most interest to them
  - o younger pupils may find talking to a teddy or doll about their grounds makes it easier to explain what is in their grounds.

- The tour findings can be recorded in different formats:
  - o written
  - o audio recordings
  - o video recordings
  - o using ICT, e.g. GIS plotting.

Activity 4: What do *you* think?

You can find out a lot of information using questionnaires, but in order to do this you need to ask the right questions in the right way. Questionnaires can be completed by pupils, staff, parents, governors or the wider community. Pupils may be able to design questionnaires themselves, or you may need adults to put them together. To a certain extent it will depend on who you are asking to complete the questionnaire.

When devising your questions, think about:

- what you want to know?
- the questions you need to ask to get useful answers
- the age and ability of those filling in the questionnaire
- the language and literacy skills of those filling in the questionnaire
- what format the questionnaire might take. For example, you could use:
    - an online survey (such as Survey Monkey)
    - a written questionnaire
    - open-ended questions. These may be harder to analyse, but allow for people to express a wider range of ideas and issues
    - images as well as or instead of words.

- how are you going to analyse the information you are gathering?
- how are you going to present the results?
- who will you present the results to?
- how are you going to use the results?

Activity 5: Let's talk!

Discussions can be very useful for finding and developing views and ideas. However, they do need to be carefully managed to be successful. These can be carried out with pupils or adults, but you are likely to be less successful if you bring both groups together into one discussion.

Sometimes a discussion can be dominated by one person, or a group of people with a specific agenda. If you know this is likely to happen then it may not be the best way of including this group – and other techniques might be more suitable.

There are, however, different ways of holding a discussion that can help it run more smoothly.

- Ask people to take on different roles within the discussion – so they are thinking about someone else's viewpoint rather than their own.
- A variation on the above is to take a specific topic with two contrasting viewpoints. Divide the group into two and give each one side of the argument to develop. Set out chairs in two concentric circles, the inner circle facing the outer circle. A member of each group sits at each chair. One side of the argument then has 60 seconds to argue their case to their opposite number. Then roles are reversed. Once this is done one of the circles moves round one place and the presentations are repeated. After the third or fourth set of presentations the groups move around again. Instead of presenting their practised viewpoint they then have to present the viewpoint they have been listening to from the other group. As a result of this debate all will have a clearer view of the two sides of the discussion and will have defined their own position more clearly. This can be good when someone doesn't like to talk within a group – when the debate is over the participants can return to their original group, give feedback on what they have heard and then a spokesperson can feed in their thoughts to the wider discussion.
- If you know one person is likely to dominate the discussion it can be a good idea to ask them to take notes of the meeting.

A 'talking stick' or similar – only the person holding an object/wearing a hat etc. can talk – means that everyone gets their say in a discussion.

Activity 6: Collecting baseline data

It is important to collect baseline data at the start of your project – this will also help you see how you have progressed as you make changes. Rather than getting everyone to look at everything within the site you can divide up into teams – whether expert teams or location specialists.

Expert teams give groups of pupils different technical aspects to undertake the research across the grounds. This might include:

- engineers to check out the range of materials used across the site
- wildlife experts to investigate whether there are good wildlife habitats across the site and if there are creatures that live in the grounds
- health and safety officers to check if the site is currently safe for use
- tree specialists to identify the trees on site and note their height, age and condition
- play researchers, to check current equipment, spaces and other features.

Location specialists divide the site up into sections and use groups of pupils to find out everything they can about one section. They then bring all this information together to create one overall plan.

- List the things that are in the space but label them as fixed, loose and living. This list of physical objects will help to give a better picture of the current outdoor area and help to inform decisions about what is possible.
- Running through the times of day, record who uses the space and for what purpose. When discussing improvements this will ensure each individual and their needs is considered in a design. Use fixed-point photography to show how a space changes over time; take a photograph of a particular space and mark where you have taken the photograph from so that you can take comparative photographs during and after the changes.

Activity 7: Using overlays

Overlays are a great way of collating information on different aspects of the school grounds. They can be used individually or combined to see how different aspects of the grounds interact.

You can create either physical overlays and/or use electronic versions – although you will need appropriate software to do this.

If you are using physical overlays then you will need tracing paper, pencils, coloured pens and masking tape as well as the tracing paper itself. You can buy large pads of tracing paper or rolls as you may want to use quite a few sheets.

Decide on the theme of each overlay, e.g. before school use, the quality and location of seating, shady spaces at a specific time of year. Make sure you note on the sheet what you are looking at and a key for your plan. Also makes sure you mark something on your overlay that matches to a key feature on your base plan so that it is easy to line up your overlays as you go through your project – it is amazing how easy it is to forget which way is up when you want to put your overlays together over your base plan!

Tips for making and using your overlays:

- Use different colours to indicate different features or different people's views:
  - Use a traffic light system for showing the condition of different features – a seat in good condition would be shown in green, in need of replacement in red and something in between in amber.
  - Use different colours for the activity or opinion of boys and girls, or different year groups – depending on which piece of information you need.
  - Use different colours for different times of year, e.g. to show shaded areas in the summer and the winter.

- You can use any symbols you like to indicate the different features but you do need to know what those symbols mean! Pupils can create their own symbols but make this clear in the keys on each overlay.
- Use masking tape to secure your overlays – this makes it easy to attach them and remove them as necessary.
- To see how different aspects interact you can put the overlays over each other. A good way of seeing how this works for up to four overlays is to tape them each along a different edge then you can lay them over your base plan one at a time, or all together.
- Pupils can work in groups on different overlays then bring all the information together, or ask more than one group to focus on the same issue or theme and combine these in the final overlay on that topic. In this way they can use their own base plans to create their group overlays and use the accurate base plan for the combined overlays.

Activity 8: Using a plan with images

Creating a giant plan of your site is a great way for everyone to be able to add ideas and comments. Not everyone will find reading a plan easy, so adding images (photos or drawings) will help ensure everyone is clear on what they are looking at. The plan can be used at different stages in the process of change and is a good way for everyone in the school to see how the project is progressing, as well as contribute to the process.

Pupils can gather images of different spaces in the grounds. Ask them either to take as many photographs as they like of different spaces and features, or to focus on features that are important to them. If you use the latter technique it is important that the images are annotated explaining why they were chosen.

For Stage 1: Where are we now? contributors should add their thoughts and feelings about the grounds, what happens there and the spaces and places they like or don't like, and why.

Activity 9: Creating a model of your site

2-D images such as plans are useful tools for looking at your grounds, and for planning the future but 3-D images are even better. Designers often use computer-aided design (CAD) programmes to create images that you can 'fly through' and get a real feel of the space that is going to be created. They can even make features within them 'grow' – which is great for the outside space as you can see what trees and other plants will look like in ten years or even 20 years.

There are simple computer programmes that schools can use to get a similar effect but using physical models means that more people can get involved in creating the grounds and more people can access, comment on and even change it.

To create a model of your grounds you will need a base plan – as big as you can – that you can lay out in a space and that can be left for some time. Adding where features are located is fairly straightforward – you can add them to scale in plan form by measuring in real life and using features to scale on your model. You may even decide that you don't need quite that level of accuracy and just want to create models of different features and locate these as accurately as possible on your plan.

If you decide to make an accurate model in all dimensions then you have a much bigger job to undertake – unless you have a very flat site. This will obviously require taking measurements around your site of features you cannot physical reach – such as the height of buildings or trees – and also the height of hills and mounds, rocks and logs, trim trails and seating. The larger your plan the easier this is but it will be quite a task whatever scale you use.

Activity 10: Creating a zoning plan

A zoning plan should be just this – an indication of where different activities could take place rather than what will be created to enable those activities to happen. Use circles, ovals and similar loose shapes to indicate on a plan where you feel the different spaces should be, such as active play, meeting places, wildlife areas. Placing these on overlays (see *Activity 7: Using overlays*) can be a good way of doing this – and allows you to try out several different layouts without destroying your original plan.

To help you think about what should go where, take a tour of your grounds (see *Activity 3: Tour of your grounds*) and think about the different spaces and what they have to offer – you may want to record your thoughts using audio or visual recording techniques.

Bear in mind that:

- some experiences or activities need to be kept separate
- people will need to cross or move around the outdoor area, perhaps to access other areas of the site
- there may be some things that you think have to be in a given space but actually could be moved – for example, would it make more sense for the car park to be where the sports pitch is, or more sense to move the location of different year groups within the school building?
- existing features/spaces could be used to develop new spaces – for example, a mature tree might be a good place to create a space for gathering a class or for socialising; the space outside the main hall might be a good place for a performance space or seating for eating outside
- spaces can be multifunctional – for example, a space for gathering a group for teaching could also be a space for parents to gather at the end of the day, a space for groups to chat.

Adult indoor activity. Draw a series of oval shapes on your overlays – one for each area you'd like to create (e.g. creative/dramatic space; natural space; physical space etc.) and label appropriately. Use them with your base plan to decide where best to site these zones. Try out different arrangements until you come up with a plan that everyone is happy with, remembering to note or photograph the various arrangements. To carry out a similar exercise with children try using representational images – for example, a bike for the physical space, a book for the quiet area.

Adult and child outdoor activity. Mark out areas for different activities with whatever you have to hand – chairs, rope, carpet tiles, boxes. Once you have decided on rough locations for your zones, sketch them out on to a copy of your base plan. Don't forget to take photographs along the way.

Activity 11: Creating a vision plan

Once you have a zoning plan (see *Activity 10: Creating a zoning plan*) you can start to create a little more detail to form a vision plan. This will show everyone where you are heading and, if you are considering large-scale changes, could be developed by a professional designer. The key to success is gathering together as much information as you can so that whoever develops your ideas understands what you are trying to do, and how your ideas have been developed.

Whether you work with a professional designer or draw up your vision plan yourselves, your vision statement and your zoning plan will help the designs to be developed. Hand this information over to a designer, together with all the other information you have collected up to this stage, or bring this information together for yourselves to use. In both cases the idea is to develop a plan of your whole site that gives an indication of the type of features you would like in your grounds. So you might want to show on the plan that you want a seating area for a class to gather, or an area for a pond and dipping platform. In this plan you will provide either a plan view or a selection of images linked to a specific space in the grounds that demonstrate the kind of feature you are working towards. This is useful to show the whole school community or a potential funder what you are trying to achieve without spending too long on details. In the next stage of the process you will be designing these areas and features in more detail but that can wait whilst you plan which part you want to develop first.

By the end of this activity you should have a vision statement and vision plan that work together to show what you are trying to achieve in your grounds and some idea of how you plan to get there. From here you will focus in on the next area you are going to develop and come up with specific design solutions and costs.

Activity 12: Creating mood boards

Mood boards help you think about the style and atmosphere you wish to create in your grounds – and also to find out what types of spaces and features you *don't* want in your grounds. These mood boards can also be used by a designer or by the school community when creating new elements for your grounds.

If you have had building work in your own home, or upgraded a room in your house, you may well have created a mood board to inspire you – gathering together images of features you have seen in magazines or other places to help inspire your final decisions about the new design.

First, gather together images of spaces and features – these may well be of school grounds but could also include other public, or private, locations. Use the internet, catalogues, magazines and this toolkit to gather images. The idea is that you are concentrating on the style and atmosphere rather than specific designs, so you could collect the following type of image:

- natural features such as woods, meadows, flowers, streams and even the beach
- modern and rustic styles of furniture
- straight benches and picnic tables
- curved, informal and moveable seating
- shelters and shade structures
- gates, fences, hedges and other boundary features
- a range of textures, materials, colours etc.
- art works of different forms
- large open spaces, including expanses of asphalt and grass
- small, intimate spaces – both natural and man-made
- loose materials for play – both natural and man-made.

In groups, pupils, staff or others look through the images (roughly A6 in size) and create two mood boards. These are large sheets of images – at least A2 in size – that provide an overall view of the type of spaces you would like for your grounds, as well as those you do not, i.e. one mood board for each.

As well as sticking images on to the boards it is valuable for comments to be written beside each image – explaining why it was chosen – so whoever looks at the mood boards understands what was valued about the features chosen; this could be layout, colour, style etc.

Activity 13: Prioritising ideas

This activity can be used to help put your ideas into order at different stages of the process, whether you are prioritising issues that need to be addressed, or trying to decide where to start your project.

1   Mark a large sheet with concentric circles – each about 20–30 cm apart.
2   Ask everyone to write down their issues/ideas on pieces of card or sticky notes. These should be placed on the outer ring of the circle. Check you only have one copy of each issue/idea.
3   Everyone moves around the outside of the circle and if they agree with one of the issues raised they move it one circle towards the centre. When everyone has been around you will see that some issues have not moved far while others are right in the middle. These are the ones to tackle first.

This method can be adapted depending on how many people are taking part. Alternatives include:

●   Using vertical lines drawn up on sheets pinned to the wall.
●   Creating a diamond shape with cards/sticky notes – those most important are placed at the top of the diamond, the least at the bottom. You are likely to find most issues come somewhere in the middle and thus the diamond shape is formed.

Activity 14: Voting on a carousel

This activity can be used to look at what pupils would like to do at playtime but can also be used by everyone to gather a range of information.

.

1   Mark three large sheets of paper each with one of the following headings 'Active', 'Quiet' and 'Other'.
2   In small groups ask pupils to think about things they would like to be able to **do** in their grounds – this could include activities they do already but should also include those they would like to do but can't now. Get them to focus on verbs rather than nouns so you get 'we want to be able to play football' not 'we want Wembley stadium'.
3   Get them to put their ideas on sticky notes so that they can be stuck appropriately to the headed paper. Check ideas aren't repeated.
4   When this is done each person in the group is given three votes (sticky dots) and they can use up to three on each sheet. They can use their votes as they like – for example, three dots on one activity if they really, really want it, or one each for three different ideas – they decide. This voting usually gets rid of any silly ideas that were put on for fun.
5   When the voting is complete it should be clear which ideas are most popular, and which are low down on the priority list. Everyone also knows that they all had the same number of votes – whether the headteacher or youngest pupil!

This activity can also be carried out with people pretending to be someone else – for example, a midday supervisor or Year 1 pupil.

Activity 15: Visiting other spaces for inspiration

Pupils, and others, may have limited experience of what is possible in school grounds but visits to other locations can help everyone in the school community understand what is possible.

- Visit other schools that have addressed similar issues to you and ask them:
  - what works well
  - what they would change
  - what they might do differently in briefing and working with a designer or contractor.

- Visit public open spaces to see what works for different users.

- Visit suppliers and manufacturers to see the variety of materials and products that are used and developed. For example, visit:
  - a quarry to select boulders
  - a nursery to learn about trees and other plants
  - a forest or manufacturer to learn about how trees can be used to create outdoor furniture.

- When visiting other spaces, take a tour asking the following questions as you go:
  - who is this space for?
  - what would you expect to do in this space?
  - what within the design makes you think this?
  - do you think the space works as it is meant to?
  - would you make any changes and if so, what would they be?
  - do you think a space like this would work in our school grounds and if not why not?

Activity 16: Life-size planning

Planning for physical change to your outdoor space can be quite daunting but using props to represent features and objects can help you plan your outdoor space.

First, decide on the location of a particular space you want to create. You are going to lay out on the ground suggested designs for your space so you will need items to do this with. To get a clear indication of how the design is going to work, the ideal scale to work on is 1:1, i.e. life-size. The range of equipment you could use might include:

- rope to mark out pathways, edges of ponds etc.
- carpet tiles or cork flooring tiles – these could be used to represent stepping stones, or seating
- flower pots or PE cones
- netting or sheets
- bamboo canes or long sticks
- pipe insulation (you'll be amazed how useful this can be!)
- pebbles, pine cones and other natural materials
- clothes dryers, chairs or other items to give height
- string and clothes pegs to help secure elements.

Essentially this is an imaginative exercise. Help the group you are working with think about what each piece of equipment could represent and both during and at the end of the activity take photographs of what they have done. You can also use this as a maths/geography activity and create a scale drawing of the plan.

Several groups should have a go and then you can compare the different solutions. You may wish to vote on which everyone likes best or discuss the designs and take the best features of each to input into the final solution. This could be a solution designed by yourselves or by a designer.

Activity 17: Developing your design brief

The aim of your design brief is to help you plan your changes or to provide the information a designer will need to develop their plans for your grounds. There is no set format to producing a design brief so you can put it together in any way you want – just make it as clear as you can to whoever is looking at it. You may decide to produce a folder or file of information, maybe supplemented with large drawings or even models, or produce a PowerPoint presentation showing the different stages you went through in gathering together information.

Everything you have done as you work through the toolkit will be useful in creating your design brief, so make sure you keep a record of your findings. The audit tool (*Part 4: Resources*) will be particularly useful in providing information about where you are now, and where your current strengths and weaknesses lie, but you will also need information about where you want to be and your own thoughts on how you could get there. Don't be too specific about what you want when you write a brief for a designer as it is their role to assess your needs into an innovative design that fits the bill. The key here is letting them know what you want to be able to *do* in your grounds, although giving them an idea of what you might like, or not like, will help them come up with solutions that are right for you. Don't forget also to give them your vision statement and any zoning or vision plans you have created.

Your brief should include information about timescales and payments where appropriate and define what you expect your designer to do, e.g. come up with a whole site plan, details of a specific area or managing the contractor implementing the work. Other, basic, technical information they need includes:

- school name, address and contact information
- base plan of the site
- details of the space to be developed
- budget
- underground services and overhead cables
- access into and around the site
- who will maintain the site and how is this done now?

You will also need to consider other issues that a designer will help you with:

- Will planning permission be required?
- What about health and safety?
- How will you go about employing a contractor and who will oversee their work?
- Are there any conservation orders or tree preservation orders related to your site?

It is a good idea to appoint your designer early on in your project. They may be able to work with you on the consultation process but it may be much more cost-effective for you to do most of this yourselves, especially with the toolkit to help you! One of the advantages in appointing a designer early on is that they can let you know exactly what information they want you to collect – and you can also discuss how they would like it presented.

Activity 18: Press release template

Issued (date) by (organiser)

Heading:

Brief heading here about your story

Begins:

The first paragraph of your press release is the most important one, and should make clear why your story is a news item. It will often include:

- What is happening?
- Where?
- When?
- Who is involved?

Then go onto explain:

- Why is it important?
- How have the events unfolded?
- Include quotes.

Photo opportunity: Give a time when a photographer can come to photograph your event – include who will be available and what will be happening.

Notes to editors:

This should include any important, relevant information designed to brief journalists rather than information for the public found in the main body of the release. Typically this will be more descriptive and detailed background information, for example a summary of the school's activities, brief history, background information about the topic, web addresses, sponsors etc. Should be printed in smaller point size, single-spaced to distinguish it from the main public message.

Contact:

For further information, photographs or to arrange interviews, please contact (name) on (telephone), (mobile), (email), (fax).

Activity 19: Skills audit template

Using ICT you can customise this template. Don't forget to acknowledge all the offers of help you get, and then collate, the information in a user-friendly way. As your project continues, don't be afraid to ask for more help. Emphasise how much has already been achieved with the help of volunteers, and make clear what additional help is needed to take the project further.

Skills survey

Your details
- Name
- Address
- Telephone
- Link with school (i.e. parent, governor, neighbour etc.)

Interests/skills – please tick the things you like to do or the jobs you are willing to undertake, indicating whether you are a 'keen beginner' or 'experienced'. Add any further comments if you wish.

Artist
- Keen beginner?   ☐
- Experienced?   ☐
- Comments

Bookkeeper
- Keen beginner?   ☐
- Experienced?   ☐
- Comments

Carpenter
- Keen beginner?   ☐
- Experienced?   ☐
- Comments

Caterer
- Keen beginner?   ☐
- Experienced?   ☐
- Comments

Childminder/crèche
- Keen beginner?   ☐
- Experienced?   ☐
- Comments

Designer
- Keen beginner? ☐
- Experienced? ☐
- Comments

DIY
- Keen beginner? ☐
- Experienced? ☐
- Comments

DJ/disco organiser
- Keen beginner? ☐
- Experienced? ☐
- Comments

First aider
- Keen beginner? ☐
- Experienced? ☐
- Comments

Fundraiser
- Keen beginner? ☐
- Experienced? ☐
- Comments

Gardener
- Keen beginner? ☐
- Experienced? ☐
- Comments

Letter writer
- Keen beginner? ☐
- Experienced? ☐
- Comments

Painter/decorator
- Keen beginner? ☐
- Experienced? ☐
- Comments

Secretary/computer operator
- Keen beginner? ☐
- Experienced? ☐
- Comments

Activity 20: Bag gardens

This activity gets pupils designing and maintaining their own 'garden' while comparing food in the UK and in an African country.

What you need

- a hessian bag per 'garden'
- large used cans or squash bottles, with top and bottom removed to make a tube of 12 cm or more in diameter
- small stones or gravel, sufficient to make a column in the middle of each bag
- mixture of topsoil and composted material, plus some well-rotted animal manure if available, to fill bags
- stakes to support bags
- chalk to mark lines on bags
- seeds or seedlings.

Preparation

- Explain how bag gardens are multistorey vegetable gardens in a sack, ideal for farmers with a limited supply of water and only a small plot of land. The central column of stones provides drainage and aeration. African families put them near their homes, where they can easily be maintained by children.
- Discuss with your pupils the best positions for the bags (sheltered, sunny, with access to water) and what plants they would like to grow (the top is great for climbing plants).

What to do

- Roll down the edges of the bag and place the tube in the bottom. Fill the tube with stones. Put a mixture of soil, compost and manure around the outside of the tube and press in slightly (but not too hard!).
- Now remove the tube. This should leave a circle of stones in the middle of the soil mix. Keep repeating step 1 and 2 until . . .
- . . . the bag is full of soil with a full column of stones at the centre. Try and keep the bag upright as you go!
- Hammer some stakes into the ground to support the bag.
- Using chalk or charcoal, mark out four or five horizontal lines around the bag, equally spaced. Carefully cut some holes in the bag, shaped like a '7' along these lines where the plants will go. Don't place them exactly above each other, but give the plants enough room to grow. The holes should be just big enough to get a hand in.
- Plant the seeds, or seedlings, into these holes and at the top of the bag. Make sure that they are held in place by the soil.
- Water the garden fairly generously at first and then water from above onto the column of stones regularly, preferably with recycled water. Use an organic feed and watch the bag produce some amazing results!

Extensions

- Decorate the bag garden with paints or fabrics.
- Compare plants under varying conditions, look at growth rates, percentage changes, fractions of original seeds becoming plants and presenting data.
- Have a crop measuring, tasting and food-making day, inviting parents along to celebrate your pupils' vegetable crop!

Activity 21: Building a shelter

Find out about shelters and their purposes then design and construct your own temporary outdoor shelter.

What you need

- blankets, curtains, bedspreads, sheets, tarpaulin, camouflage material, corrugated plastic sheets etc.
- straw bales
- evergreen prunings
- pegs
- bamboo canes, hazel and/or willow sticks
- long and short ropes, string, strong elastic bands, masking tape
- pulleys
- scissors.

Preparation

- Discuss and explore the constructions of shelters by looking at books and websites illustrating the variety and diversity of shelter building around the world.
- Get the pupils to each design a shelter on paper – they should think about its purpose, and label it accordingly.
- Gather materials – ask pupils to bring in what they have at home that might be suitable; make links with your local Scout group, forest school, woodland management team, scrap store etc.

What to do

- Go outside and identify good spots for shelter building – up against a fence or wall, between two shrubs, under a tree.
- Make all the materials readily available and get the pupils in groups to construct their shelter.
- Once the shelters have been built, discuss ways in which to evaluate each one. For example, is it waterproof? How can you prove this? Does it enhance the environment? How stable is it?

Extensions

- Use giant construction kits to make shelters and explore how these compare, especially in terms of stability.
- Give the pupils a stack of old newspapers. Is it possible to build a framework and covering from just these?
- Invite a professional such as an architect to visit and talk about design and construction.

Activity 22: Building homes for minibeasts

Find out where the minibeasts in your school grounds live, and create new habitats to attract more minibeasts.

What you need

- hand lens or similar to spot and magnify minibeasts
- record sheet (see over page)
- leaf litter
- old wood – branches and logs
- bundles of twigs
- old rocks and bricks
- old plant pots
- a plastic bucket.

Preparation

- Go on a minibeast hunt to find out what kind of habitats minibeasts like most.
- Identify key features of these habitats – for example dark, sheltered, damp (but not too wet) and mouldy – and fill in a record sheet.
- Discuss how these habitats can be recreated.

What to do

Divide pupils into groups. They should go into the grounds and identify two suitable spaces where new homes for minibeasts could be built and left undisturbed. These could be marked on a map of the school grounds. Then provide the groups with the necessary material so they can construct different types of habitats themselves in their chosen spaces. They could, for example:

- Build a log pile – leave a pile of logs and dead branches in one corner – preferably under some trees or shrubs where it's shady. Leave the wood to rot.
- Make an insect box – take a bundle of twigs and tie together with a piece of string. Hang under the branch of a tree or to a railing.
- Fill an old plant pot with leaf debris, turn upside down and position somewhere damp.
- Create an informal rockery from a pile of rocks and bricks – especially good for insects in the winter months.
- Make some holes in the sides of a plastic bucket and fill with wood chips and soil. Leave it somewhere quiet where it won't be disturbed, topping up with soil every now and again. This is a great habitat for stag beetles as well as lots of other insects.
- Plant a small fruit tree in a pot and leave the fruit to rot.

Extensions

- While on their minibeast hunt the pupils could collect as many examples of minibeasts as possible and sort them into groups. The best way to do this is by counting their legs:
  - o **no legs**: worms, slugs and snails
  - o **six legs**: insects such as beetles, wasps, flies, butterflies and earwigs
  - o **eight legs**: spiders and harvestmen
  - o **14 legs**: slaters and woodlice
  - o **more than 14**: millipedes and centipedes.

- Produce geographical presentations of their findings from their minibeast hunt.
- Take photographs and or/make observational drawings or clay models of the minibeasts they find and create an exhibition.
- Use colour swatches to identify the colour of the animals and try to recreate that colour with paint, exploring why their animal may have adapted to be a certain colour.
- Talk about what other animals may come to these habitats to feed on the minibeasts.

Activity 23: Constructing a rainwater collection system

The purpose of this activity is to design and construct a system that collects rainwater, investigate ways in which this water can be used and reduce water consumption.

What you need

- water butt(s)
- lengths of guttering
- screws
- drills
- hacksaws
- lengths of hose.

Preparation

- Investigate water use within the school and school grounds. How, for example, is the pond topped up? Where does the water come from for watering the plants/vegetable beds? Are there outside taps? Any existing water butts?
- Identify existing water-saving systems, if there are any, and evaluate their success. Is there a water meter, for example, that calculates water use? Is this monitored within the school?
- Visit local gardens, explore websites etc. and find out about commonly used rainwater collection systems.

What to do

- Get the students to identify the most suitable place for constructing a rain collection system. Encourage them to consider important points, such as how the water will be transported to where it is needed; safety; ease of construction etc.
- Get the students to design their own rainwater collection system. Encourage them to think about materials, stability, water flow, safety, ease of use etc. They could do this on paper and/or make a scale model.
- Provide students with the materials needed and supervise the construction of their rainwater collection system. They could work in groups, taking responsibility for different parts of the construction (i.e. connecting the butt to the guttering, positioning and securing the water butt, fixing the tap).

Extensions

- Once the rainwater system is in place, explore how best to transport the water to where it is needed. For example, would a system of hosepipes work? Could a timer be incorporated so plants could be watered during the school holidays? What about hand pumps?
- Evaluate the success of the water collection system. For example, explore ways of measuring how much water is collected and how much is used and, if possible, compare meter readings to assess how water consumption has been affected.

Activity 24: Healthy?

Get pupils thinking about different aspects of health and carry out a healthy school grounds audit to identify areas for improvement.

What you need

- Each pupil, or group of pupils, will need a copy of a sheet posing the following questions:

  o Where in our school grounds . . . Can I be active?

  Do I feel happy?

  Can I sit quietly?

  Can I be with friends?

  Helps me learn about healthy eating?

  o How can we make our school grounds healthier?

- Clipboards will be useful.
- Digital cameras can add interest to this activity.
- You might want to produce a wall display or word-processed report of the pupils' findings.

Preparation

- Introduce as many of the different types of health – physical, emotional, mental, social, spiritual – as you think suitable for the age and ability of your pupils. Talk about things that they do which are good or bad for their health.

What to do

- Divide pupils into small groups.
- Start with all the pupils in one area, discussing how that area is good or bad for different types of health – e.g. a woodland area might be good for physical health if it is a favourite place for playing 'chase' games, or good for spiritual and emotional health if it is somewhere you can sit quietly among nature.
- You could ask groups to explore the whole grounds, or send them to the specific areas to be discussed.
- Ask children to write or draw pictures on their record sheet about the places where they can be active, feel happy etc.
- Alternatively they could take photos to create a wall display.
- Another way to carry out an audit is to ask groups to find one place in the grounds that they think is good for one or more types of health, and explain why they chose it. You might want to make them look at specific types of health, or choose different types of health for different groups according to ability – spiritual and social health are harder concepts than physical health.
- Pupils should also suggest one or more ways to make your school grounds better for health.

Extensions

- Pupils could present their analysis to decision-makers – e.g. the headteacher or governors.
- Make sure that pupils see their recommendations are taken seriously – if they are not acted upon, explain why a different decision has been taken.
- Pupils could help plan a school grounds improvement project to implement their suggestions.

More useful organisations
(see also *Part 3: Heading towards your vision*)

Anti-Bullying Alliance – www.anti-bullyingalliance.org.uk
Architecture and Design Scotland – www.ads.org.uk/smarterplaces
Arts Council – www.artscouncil.org.uk
Arts Council Northern Ireland – www.artscouncil-ni.org
Arts Wales – www.artswales.org.uk
The Association of Gardens Trusts – www.gardenstrusts.org.uk

Beat Bullying – www.beatbullying.org
Botanical Society of the British Isles – www.bsbi.org.uk
British Association of Landscape Industries (BALI) – www.bali.co.uk
British Council for School Environments – www.bcse.uk.net
British Ecological Society – www.britishecologicalsociety.org
The British Herpetological Society – www.tbhs.org

CABE at the Design Council (England) – www.designcouncil.org.uk
Common Ground – www.commonground.org.uk
The Conservation Volunteers – www.tcv.org.uk
Council for Learning Outside the Classroom – www.lotc.org.uk
Countryside Council for Wales – www.ccw.gov.uk
Countryside Education Trust – www.cet.org.uk

Department for Education (Northern Ireland) – www.deni.gov.uk
Directory of Social Change – www.dsc.org.uk

Eden Project – www.edenproject.com
Education Scotland – www.educationscotland.gov.uk
Education Wales – www.learning.wales.gov.uk
Extended Schools – www.direct.giv.uk/parents/childcare

Farming and Countryside Education (FACE) – www.facr-online.org.uk
Forest Education Initiative – www.foresteducation.org
Free Play Network – www.freeplaynetwork.org.uk
Froglife – www.froglife.org

Garden Organic – www.gardenorganic.org.uk
Global Footprints – www.globalfootprints.org.uk
Groundwork – www.groundwork.org.uk
Growing Schools – www.growingschools.org.uk

Healthy Living in Scotland – http://www.scotland.gov.uk/Topics/Education/
    Schools/HLivi/
Healthy Schools in England – http://www.education.gov.uk/schools/pupilsupport/
    pastoralcare/a0075278/healthy-schools
Healthy Schools Northern Ireland – http://www.healthpromotionagency.org.uk/
    work/hpschools/menu.htm

International School Grounds Alliance – www.greenschoolyards.org

Landlife – www.wildflower.co.uk
Landscape Institute – www.landscapeinstitute.org.uk
Learning through Landscapes – www.ltl.org.uk

National Association of Field Studies Officers – www.nafso.org.uk
National Confederation of Parent Teachers Associations – www.ncpta.org.uk
Natural England – www.naturalengland.org.uk

Open Air Laboratories – www.opalexplorenature.org
Ordnance Survey – www.ordnancesurvey.co.uk
Outdoor learning in Scotland – http://www.educationscotland.gov.uk/learning
    teachingandassessment/approaches/outdoorlearning/index.asp

Plantlife Scotland – www.plantlife.org.uk/scotland
Playboard Northern Ireland – www.playboard.org
Playlink – www.playlink.org
Play England – www.playengland.org.uk
Play Scotland – www.playscotland.org
Play Wales – www.playwales.org.uk
Pond Conservation – www.pondconservation.org.uk

The Royal Horticultural Society – www.rhs.org.uk
Royal Society for Prevention of Accidents – www.rospa.com
RSPB – www.rspb.org.uk

Scottish Arts – www.scottisharts.org.uk
Scottish Biodiversity Forum – www.biodiversityscotland.gov.uk
Scottish Natural Heritage – www.snh.org.uk
Scottish Parent Teacher Council – www.sptc.info
Sense Scotland – www.sensescotland.org.uk
The Sensory Trust – www.sensorytrust.org.uk
Sustainable Schools Alliance – www.sustainable-schools-alliance.org.uk/
Sustainable Schools at Sustainability and Environmental Education (SEEd) –
    www.se-ed.co.uk/sustainable-schools/

Thrive – www.thrive.org.uk
21st Century Schools (Wales) – www.21stcenturyschools.org

Welsh Network of Healthy Schools Schemes – http://wales.gov.uk/topics/health/
    improvement/schools/schemes/?lang=en
The Wildlife Trusts – www.wildlifetrusts.orgThe Woodland Trust www.woodlandtrust.
    org.uk

Bibliography

Browning, L. and Robinson, F. (2011) *Naturally Inclusive*. Winchester: Learning through Landscapes.

Dillon, J., Morris, M., O'Donnell, L., Reid, A., Rickinson, M. and Scott, W. (2005) *Engaging and Learning with the Outdoors – The Final Report of the Outdoor Classroom in a Rural Context Action Research Project*. Slough: National Foundation for Educational Research.

Fisher, K. (2005) *Research into Identifying Effective Learning Environments*. London: Rubida Research Pty Ltd.

Gill, T. (2011) *Children and Nature: A Quasi Systematic Review of the Empirical Evidence*. London: Greater London Authority.

Gray, P. (2012) 'Free Play is Essential for Normal Emotional Development.' *Freedom to Learn* June 21. Available online: http://www.psychologytoday.com [accessed 25 March 2013].

Groves, L. (2011) *Natural Play: Making a Difference to Children's Learning and Wellbeing*. A Longitudinal Study of the Forestry Commission Scotland. Glasgow: Forestry Commission Scotland.

Ipsos MORI (2008) *Teachers Omnibus 2007*. London: Ipsos MORI.

Ipsos MORI (2010) *Teachers Omnibus 2009*. London: Ipsos MORI.

King's College London (2011) *Understanding the Diverse Benefits of Learning in Natural Environments*. London: King's College London.

Learning through Landscapes (1994) *Special Places, Special People*. Godalming: WWF UK.

Learning through Landscapes (2003) *National School Grounds Survey*. Winchester: Learning through Landscapes.

Learning through Landscapes in London (2003) *Grounds for Celebration: Measuring Impact of School Grounds Projects in London*. London: Learning through Landscapes.

Louv, R. (2010) *Last Child in the Woods*. New York: Atlantic Books.

Ludvigsen, A., Creegan, C. and Mills, H. (2005) *Let's Play Together: Play and Inclusion – Evaluation of Better Play Round Three*. Ilford: Barnardos Policy and Research Unit.

Natural England (2009) *Childhood and Nature: A Survey on Changing Relationships with Nature across the Generations*. Warboys: England Marketing.

Natural England (2012) *Learning in the Natural Environment: Review of Social and Economic Benefits and Barriers*. London: Natural England.

The Royal Horticultural Society (2010) *Gardening in Schools: A Vital Tool for Children's Learning*. London: RHS.

Short Science Reviews (2007) 'Foresight Tackling Obesities: Future Choices.' *Obesity Reviews* 8(s1)v–210. Available online: http://www.foresight.gov.uk [accessed 25 March 2013].

YouGov (2010) *Free Schools: Do They Make Education Standards Better or Worse, or Do They Make No Difference?* September 2011. Available online: http://yougov.co.uk/news/2012/09/11/free-schools-do-they-make-education-standards-bett/ [accessed 25 March 2013].